U.S. GUIDE
TO
LITERARY LANDMARKS

By
Geri and Eben Bass

j.pohl associates

Second Printing, October 1985
Copyright © 1984 by Geri and Eben Bass

Published By

J. POHL ASSOCIATES
461 Spring Run Road
Coraopolis, PA 15108

ISBN 0-939332-09-4

Cover Design By T. W. McKenzie
Mark Twain Study
Elmira, N.Y.

TABLE OF CONTENTS

INTRODUCTION

This book expresses our mutual love affair with American literature. Since poets, essayists and fiction writers are real people who live or lived in real places, we believe that persons and places belong to the writing that comes of them. True, authors may not of themselves be extraordinary, nor may the places where they lived or traveled to have interest by themselves. It is the combination that matters. For example, one gets a sense of the physical scale of things by a visit to Concord, and although Walden Pond is partly spoiled with public bathing and crowds of people, at least the cabin site is marked with a sign announcing "Where I lived . . ." Amherst is no longer a village, but the Dickinson house, as a national landmark, cannot be changed. The place and whatever fleeting sense of the person it may still contain in no way "are" the literature, but it is a mistake not to realize that the two had everything to do with the making of the one. It is the mysterious coming together that counts: Twain and his great river, Cather and the silhouette of a plow, magnified against the setting sun.

Why we chose these particular writers and places is part of the love affair. Other persons might have added other authors, but most of the ones who have caught our concerns are likely to have done the same for others. Few living authors are included here for two reasons. An author deserves the degree of privacy that he or she requires in order to be a writer, and privacy is not served by giving street addresses or residences of working writers. Also, with the wealth of interesting and important living American authors, it would be difficult to choose among the many to put together a book small enough to carry when traveling on one's own literary pilgrimage. Once that process is begun, to be sure, it becomes habit-forming, and like other good habits, it is worth cultivating.

Our book is meant as a travel companion, a guide to enable discoveries which, if not already made, deserve to be. There are indeed scholarly books that are also a joy to read — Arlin Turner's on Hawthorne, Justin Kaplan's on Whitman — but our aim was not to be specialized or scholarly, only to share some particular pleasures with those who read and enjoy the great literature of our country.

America is beginning more and more to honor its writers through national landmark plaques and through local, regional and national organizations that preserve the visible part of a writer's heritage. One can get that sense, as we did, from a summer at Bread Loaf, Vermont, which still preserves its feeling for Frost. Each year the Hemingway Society stages conferences — this year in Madrid, or as in its first year, at the Kennedy Center in Boston. Willa Cather is celebrated annually in Red Cloud, Nebraska; William Faulkner at Rowan Oak, Oxford, Mississippi; and Washington Irving's presence is felt at Sunnyside, Tarrytown, New York. In one celebration at Carmel, California, for Robinson Jeffers, Judith Anderson stood at the top of Hawk Tower and spoke some of Jeffers' poems. So place is also part of the writer's experience, which in turn becomes literature. The trick is to see how the end result is, and is more than, its place of origin. The visitor to any landmark must indulge his imagination accordingly, or he will miss the whole point of the exercise.

America has also come of age in that good, permanent editions of our worthy authors are now being published. All too often in the past, important works were out of print or published in formats that were only somewhat better than the newspaper typesetting of Hank Morgan's protegés in Twain's *Connecticut Yankee*. Beginning in 1979, Library of America started to publish fine editions of important American authors. In the alumni magazine *Pitt*, May 1984, Dr. Robert Gale, Professor of English at the University of Pittsburgh, expresses real joy at the results. Issued by Library of America in May 1982 were works by Hawthorne, Melville, Stowe, and Whitman. A dozen more have appeared since, by Howells, London, Twain, Adams, Emerson, Irving, and James. Viking Press distributes these editions to book stores; Time-Life, through subscription. Each book is an example of fine craftsmanship.

Not so many years ago, the *Times* (of London, but recently purchased by an Australian) queried, "*Is* there an American literature?" Indeed there is, though if like Twain's novel *Huckleberry Finn* it was a long time "a-borning," part of the fault is due to its having been left in schoolrooms and academic libraries. But more and more Americans are meeting their literature on its own terms rather than those of James Thurber's Miss Groby, who pounced so ardently on every Container for the Thing Contained in literature that she scared away most of her students. We are becoming less self-conscious about our great authors, and appreciate them for who they are, where they lived, and to what purpose. A literary landmark is a part of that.

No book is done without the help of others. We are especially grateful to the following persons and societies for furnishing information and help that have aided in making this a better description of some American literary landmarks that deserve to be remembered. We thank Dr. May Ireland, Professor Emerita of English, Lock Haven University, Pennsylvania; Mr. Thaddeus Hurd, Clyde, Ohio; Mr. Glen Giffen, Clyde, Ohio; Miss Marie Rossi, Public Library, Sewickley, Pennsylvania; The Pearl S. Buck Foundation, Inc., Perkasie, Pennsylvania; The Thomas Wolfe Memorial, Asheville, North Carolina; The Carl Sandburg Home, N.H.S., Flat Rock, North Carolina; Mrs. Lucille Tomko, Carnegie Library, Pittsburgh; The Historical Society of Elmira, New York.

NEW ENGLAND

LOUISA MAY ALCOTT
1832 — 1888
Orchard House, Concord, Massachusetts

Although Louisa May Alcott was born in Germantown, Pennsylvania, where her father conducted a school, the family is more permanently associated with Concord, Massachusetts. In Orchard House Louisa May Alcott, popular children's novelist, lived with her parents and sisters. Located on the corner of Alcott and Lexington Roads in Concord, it is the place where Louisa's *Little Women* was written. Bronson Alcott, head of the family, was a Transcendentalist lecturer, writer, and friend of Hawthorne and Emerson, but his enterprises never succeeded financially; and thus it remained for courageous Louisa to be the family breadwinner. Secretly in love with Henry David Thoreau, Louisa was bound to be disappointed with any return of affection from him, though Thoreau sometimes lectured at the primitive wooden School of Philosophy that Bronson had built behind Orchard House for Transcendentalist believers. Their ideas ranged from Bronson Alcott's eating only "aspiring" vegetables, rather than root types, to the sublimities of Ralph Waldo Emerson's Oversoul and his ideas on progressive education. Although Emerson, Thoreau, Hawthorne and the Alcotts were all Concord personalities at the time of the Anti-Slavery Movement, each used his or her own way to oppose slavery. Louisa, who had been involved with the abolitionists, also joined the struggle for women's rights. As an activist, she tried to encourage a following in Concord, but she had many discouraging moments. Nevertheless, she was the first female to cast a ballot in Concord, even if her vote was not counted.

EMILY DICKINSON
1830 — 1886
Family Home, Amherst, Massachusetts

The home of Emily Dickinson is on Main Street, Amherst, Massachusetts. Qualifying for Noah Webster's definition of a "mansion" (a large house with at least four chimneys), it was sold out of the family for a time and bought back in 1855 by Edward Dickinson, congressman, man of affairs, and father of Emily. Emily's room was upstairs, left front, where some of her personal effects may still be seen: her bed, her paisley shawl, her hat box, and some of her tiny white dresses. Furniture from her bedroom and her piano along with her manuscript poems are at Harvard University's Houghton Library. The Amherst House is now used as the residence of the chaplain of Amherst College. Emily attended Amherst Academy and spent one year at Mount Holyoke College. When she was young, she kept up a busy social life and made many strong friendships. Later as a more private person, she enjoyed the company of special friends. One of her poems remarks: "The Soul selects her own Society." This remarkable woman poet was being introspective when she wrote: "I'm nobody; who are you?" Emily loved her home where she lived with her sister Lavinia after her parents' deaths. She enjoyed baking bread, tending her lovely flower garden, and taking care of the house, as well as "publishing" her poems in small handwritten packets that were seen by no one until after her death.

The Path Next Door, Amherst

"The Path Next Door" led from the Dickinson house to that of Emily's brother Austin and his wife Susan. As one of Emily's confidantes, Susan often received notes and poems sent to her in a basket with flowers or pastries, the deliveries being made by her own children. A fancier of wildlife, Emily kept a small conservatory for wildflowers as well as an outdoor garden, and she was fond of the living things she observed in the meadow across the road from her home. Her poems, less than ten of which were published in her lifetime (and anonymously) are replete with nature subjects. Written originally without titles on odd bits of paper, these witty and enlightening verses express intense feelings. Fortunately, her sister Lavinia disobeyed the request Emily made late in life that all of the poems be destroyed.

Cemetery, Amherst

When Emily Dickinson died in 1886, her casket was carried out of the rear door of her home, across the fields, to the family burial plot which was surrounded by an iron fence to keep out wandering cattle. On her grave marker are her name, birth and death dates, and the simple phrase "Called Back" — as if quaintly to express her belief in the resurrection, even though many of her poems suggest doubts about her religious faith. On his deathbed, being asked if he had made his peace with God, Thoreau (with characteristic wit) remarked that he was unaware they had ever quarreled. We have no such record of Emily Dickinson's last words, but her poems express intense curiosity about the last words, signs or gestures of dying persons who, presumably, were about to meet God. As with the metaphysical poets Donne and Herbert, Dickinson tests her senses and intuition for evidence of the divine presence and is seldom at ease with what she finds. But the tenseness we feel there should not be mistaken for mere disbelief. Her "Tomorrow is composed of nows" means, among other things, that immortality is the sum of those deeply and briefly felt moments that it is a poet's task to capture and record.

T. S. ELIOT
1888 — 1965
Cape Ann, Massachusetts

The brilliant intellectualism of Eliot's poetry and the forcefulness of his literary criticism made him the most influential Anglo-American writer for an entire generation. Born in St. Louis, Missouri, Thomas Stearns Eliot was the product of genteel upbringing. Educated at Harvard, in his graduate years he discovered the poems of Donne and the plays of Elizabethans and Jacobeans; these were to be hallmarks in his later critical essays. When Eliot's "The Love Song of J. Alfred Prufrock" was published in 1915 in *Poetry*, a new style of verse was created, and Eliot became a serious poet rather than following the career of a philosopher, which had been his first intent. Ezra Pound, an expatriate American who had helped Robert Frost win recognition when Frost came to England, was even more instrumental in Eliot's gaining attention as a poet. *The Waste Land* (1921), written after Eliot had convalesced from a nervous

collapse, clearly established him as the spokesperson and pace setter for a new poetry that compounded symbolism, obscure literary allusions, and a deliberately fragmented structure that expressed the fragmentation of Western culture after World War I. In reassembling those fragments in his further criticism and poems, Eliot declared himself a royalist in politics, an anglo-catholic by faith and a classicist in literature. Settling permanently in England in 1915, he became an employee of the foreign division of Lloyd's Bank; the efforts consumed in this daily work, he said, left him time to write only the best poetry and criticism of which he was capable. Much of his urbanity and self-assurance is styled after Matthew Arnold, but his substance is beyond Arnold's range. Eliot sought the free rhythms of colloquial speech in his poems, he tapped the sources of racial memory in his use of myth, and he made extraordinary demands on his readers' knowledge of obscure and varied literary and philosophical works that match the demands that Ezra Pound, his mentor, made of his readers. *The Dry Salvages* (1941), published as part of *The Four Quartets* (1943), derives its name from the narrow rim of rocks off the coast of Cape Ann (East Gloucester, Massachusetts): supposedly the name was once *trois sauvages* (three Indians). Another American place associated with Eliot is Princeton, New Jersey. He lived at 14 Alexander Street from 1948-1949 while at the Institute for Advanced Study, and his sophisticated verse drama *The Cocktail Party* was written at Fuld Hall, Institute headquarters. The currently popular musical play, first in London and now New York, *Cats*, had its surprising origin in Eliot's *Old Possum's Book of Practical Cats* (1939), fanciful verse written for children.

RALPH WALDO EMERSON
1803 — 1882
Portrait

Ralph Waldo Emerson, sage of Concord and classic essayist, is memorialized in this daguerreotype of 1854 that can be seen in the Emerson House, Concord, Massachusetts. Making daguerreotypes, an early form of photography, is the trade of the bright young man Holgrave who courts Phoebe in Hawthorne's novel *The House of the Seven Gables*. Originally a Unitarian minister, Emerson argued himself out of the church altogether and helped to develop the Transcendentalist philosophy that stems from German Romantic philosophers like Kant and that won the admiration of Thomas Carlyle. Emerson's idealistic views countermanded the dour old Puritan doctrine of predestination and original sin. Indeed, he argues that the only sin is the personal failure to find that spark of divinity which is a part of one's natural self and to fulfill it to its greatest potential.

The Ralph Waldo Emerson House in Concord, located on Cambridge Turnpike at Lexington Road, is within walking distance of Orchard House, home of the Alcotts, Transcendentalist neighbors. During the time when Emerson was traveling in Europe, his close friend Henry David Thoreau "looked after" the Emerson house by doing such chores as filling the woodbox near the back door of the house, fixing furniture, trimming trees, and gardening. In the well-known family living room still sit Emerson's green rocker and his wife's red rocker on either side of the fireplace. Many friends visited in this room, especially the Transcendental Club that included such members as Theodore Parker, Bronson Alcott and Margaret Fuller. The contrast between Emerson and his most famous friend, Thoreau, is remarkable. Emerson was the mentor whom Thoreau came to equal and in some ways rival. For Thoreau, Concord was world enough to travel in; for Emerson, Boston and Europe were space to move in physically and intellectually. Writers as various as Channing, Whittier, Longfellow, James, Harte, and Sumner visited Emerson here; and after Walt Whitman came here from New York to see Emerson, Walt was to be (privately) "greeted at the beginning of a great career" by Emerson — a tribute Whitman ill-advisedly circulated to the embarrassment of both Emerson and himself.

Emerson House, Study

The original furnishings of the Study of Emerson are now in the Museum of the Antiquarian Society (for fire protection), and replicas can be seen in the original setting, the Emerson home. The collection of books and his own writing represent Emerson's unexpected and unlikely triumph over adversity. Emerson's father died when the boy was only eight years old: the mother was left with little or no means to educate her five young sons. Ralph Waldo attended Boston Latin School, the Latin school of Concord, and then Harvard College, where from 1817-1821 he had a "scholarship" in return for doing work; but he showed no great promise. Not until eight years later with his decision to leave the ministry is there anything remarkable about Emerson; but his "Divinity School Address" (1838), influenced by religious non-conformists like George Fox, Luther and Carlyle, is explosive in its challenge to religious orthodoxy. The Emerson Study was the scene of his meetings and discussions with his literary and philosophical peers.

Emerson House, Dining Room

The Emerson Dining Room is large and pleasant, the double windows looking across the fields in the direction of Walden Pond, subject of the best-known book of Henry David Thoreau. The large carpeted room has an attractive fireplace and a comfortable rocker for reading while one is warmed by the fire. Family pictures create an intimate feeling. The double dining room table is accounted for by the fact that when Emerson married a second time in 1835 (his first wife died in 1831), the couple discovered that they owned identical dining room tables; these were placed side by side and could be opened out into a splendid banquet-size setting.

The Old North Bridge, Concord

The Old North Bridge (now the latest of a series of replicas) crosses the Concord River at the place where provincial soldiers confronted British regulars on April 19, 1775. The colonial soldiers began to cross the bridge because they were alarmed at the sight of the British burning supplies; the British fired upon them, but hostilities lasted only two or three minutes. This was the first encounter of the American Revolution, "the shot heard round the world," as Emerson describes the event in his "Concord Hymn": "By the rude bridge that arched the flood/ Their flag to April's breeze unfurled." The monument of the Minute Man on the west side of the bridge contains the text of Emerson's "Concord Hymn."

Emerson's Grave, Sleepy Hollow Cemetery

Emerson's Grave marker, an unusually-shaped mass of granite with a bronze plaque, is found in the Sleepy Hollow Cemetery of Concord, Bedford Street. Nearby is the small, simple marker for Thoreau, along with others for the Thoreau family members. Another plot honors the Hawthorne family. Also in the area are the Alcott plot and that of William Ellery Channing.

ROBERT FROST
1874 — 1963
Pinkerton Academy, West Derry, New Hampshire

Living with his wife Elinor and their growing family on a small, run-down thirty-acre farm in West Derry, New Hampshire (South Main Street and Rockingham Road), Robert Frost tried in the first years of this century to be both farmer and schoolteacher. But both enterprises came second to the writing of poetry. Milking his only cow at midnight so that he could spend time with his poems did not impress Frost's farmer neighbors. Nevertheless, other townspeople were so impressed with his poetry reading that he was offered a teaching position at Pinkerton Academy. His classroom was in the second floor tower room, where his creative and unpredictable ways with students made him their great friend. His principal called Frost one of the best teachers in New Hampshire, and Frost was later appointed psychology and education teacher at Plymouth State Normal School.

West-Running Brook is not far from the Derry farmhouse, which Frost sold in 1912 in order to go to England where he knew no one but where he hoped to make his poems known. The Brook seems nondescript enough running through a culvert under the highway and marked by a highway department sign, but in the wooded setting in which Frost places it in his poem it takes on deep significance. "West-Running Brook" is the greatest of Frost's marriage poems, and it contains echoes of classic poets like Lucretius, of whom Frost was especially fond. The scheme of contraries, of life running down while yet being urged back to its primal source, emerges from the domestic differences somehow resolved between man and wife, just as the sometimes stormy marriage of Robert and Elinor Frost was somehow resolved into a deep, lasting matter that ended only with Elinor's death in 1938. They had shared valedictorian honors in 1892 as graduates from high school in Lawrence, Massachusetts, and the resolving of marriage stresses is one of the great themes of Frost's poems. Little wonder that he was inconsolable when Elinor died.

Amherst House

With a very meagre publishing record in America, Robert Frost's real career as a poet began in England with the friendly help of Ezra Pound. When Frost returned to America after a stay in England, *A Boy's Will* and *North of Boston* (both published in England) began to receive the good reviews these books of poems deserved. During the next forty years Frost became the most widely honored of American poets through his success in reaching large reading and listening audiences who understood Frost's regional language and who found his subjects significant and original. Though primarily a poet, Frost also distinguished himself as a teacher, reader of his own poetry, and sometime lecturer. As poet in residence he was associated longest with Amherst College (1917-1920, 1923-1928, 1949), but he also held honored posts at Michigan, Harvard, and Dartmouth. The white Victorian house where the Frosts were living in 1938 when Elinor died is located at 43 Sunset Avenue in Amherst, Massachusetts.

The Frost Memorial Library, which contains original manuscript materials of both Robert Frost and Emily Dickinson, is located on the campus of Amherst College. President John F. Kennedy laid the cornerstone of the building. Perhaps the most touching moment during the inauguration of the young President in January 1961 was Frost's recitation of his poem written for the occasion, "The Gift Outright." To express his appreciation James Reston wrote in the New York *Times*, "Every time Robert Frost comes to town the Washington Monument stands up a little straighter."

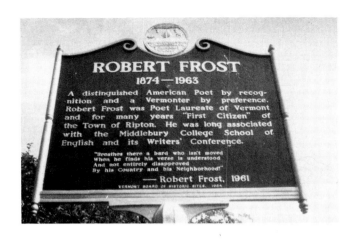

Ripton and Bread Loaf, Vermont

In 1922, Robert Frost helped to organize the Bread Loaf Writers' Conference at Middlebury, Vermont. Associated with Middlebury College, the Conference has been held annually thereafter on Bread Loaf Mountain at facilities the College uses in winter as a ski resort. Frost's friend Louis Untermeyer was another founder of the Conference that set a pattern to be widely imitated by many other such summer enterprises for writers. Frost usually participated in the summer conferences at Bread Loaf, and several times at the counterpart group in Boulder, Colorado. Nearby Bread Loaf in Ripton, Vermont, Frost bought the Homer Noble Farm to lead a private life and to be near Bread Loaf. His dear friends, Ted and Kathleen Morrison, agreed to rent the farmhouse. Professor Morrison taught at Harvard, and his wife became Frost's secretary. Frost, for writer's privacy, lived in a log cabin a short distance away, with his dog for company. When guests arrived, he and the Morrisons would visit with them in the farmhouse or on occasion Frost would take them to his cabin to talk for many hours.

31

NATHANIEL HAWTHORNE
1804 — 1864
Birthplace, Salem, Massachusetts

Born on Independence Day in 1804 in this house in Salem, Massachusetts, Nathaniel Hawthorne inherited a Puritan consciousness (an ancestor had been a judge at the Salem witch trials). After finishing college, Hawthorne spent a dozen years steeping himself in New England history and writing about it. Thereafter, he made only mildly successful efforts to publish his tales; there were few American journals and publishing houses. Not until 1837, with the publication of his *Twice Told Tales*, did his work win any real public notice, both in America and England. At this time Hawthorne wrote of his solitary efforts in the upstairs room of his mother's Salem house: "In this dismal and sordid chamber FAME was won." The Hawthorne house has recently been moved to a location near the famous House of Seven Gables in Salem.

Old Manse, Concord
Monument Street at the Old North Bridge

The Old Manse, ancestral home of the Emersons built in 1769 in Concord, Massachusetts, was the home of the Rev. William Emerson; and his son Ralph Waldo lived there when he wrote his essay "Nature" (1836). Novelist Nathaniel Hawthorne brought his young bride Sophia there in 1842, and in the same room in which Emerson wrote "Nature" Hawthorne later wrote his *Mosses From an Old Manse* (1846), a collection of tales. The Hawthornes spent four blissful years at the Old Manse, probably the happiest years of their marriage. On an upstairs window with her diamond engagement ring Sophia scratched her name along with a brief dialogue between herself and Nathaniel. Beside the house runs the small Concord River, subject of Thoreau's book *A Week on the Concord and Merrimack Rivers* (1849). Crossing the River is the "rude bridge" (many times since reconstructed) that Emerson describes in his poem "Concord Hymn."

Because of Hawthorne's help to local Salem Democrats, he was given the post of Surveyor of the Port of Salem in 1846. Salem was by this time a declining seaport, its earlier promise having been overtaken by rivals like thriving Boston. When the Whig Party came to power in 1849, Hawthorne lost his job at the Custom House; political controversy followed in local papers about the spoils system; and Hawthorne's mother died at the end of the summer. Caught in the emotional turmoil caused by these events, he began work on *The Scarlet Letter*, whose publication in 1850 caused a sensation in both England and America. Critics both here and abroad now recognized Hawthorne as the finest American novelist.

Hawthorne's Desk, Custom House

In a long introduction to *The Scarlet Letter*, Hawthorne took revenge on the local politicians of Salem who had cost him his job at the Custom House. Though mild by some standards, these attacks were resented by the persons involved. The Introduction describes the snail-paced activity at the Custom House, where Hawthorne pretends to have discovered old documents about the sin and punishment of one Hester Prynne, and along with these an ancient embroidered relic, the scarlet letter itself. Hawthorne's writing desk and stool can still be seen in the Custom House. Biographers have found that he was less shy and withdrawn than he represented himself to be in his writings. The intense characterization of Hester Prynne, at once sympathetic and judgmental, has something to do with the disparagement his mother faced from her Salem in-laws when her first child was born only seven months after her marriage to Hawthorne's father. The father, a sea-captain, died in Surinam (Dutch Guiana) when Nathaniel was only four years old.

Hawthorne Cottage, Lenox

A replica of the Red Cottage in which Hawthorne lived for a year and a half (1850-1851) at Lenox, Massachusetts, this structure located on Hawthorne Road is now used by students of the Tanglewood Music Festival. The Hawthorne family enjoyed the beautiful Berkshire summer and endured the severe winter weather. But after a time Hawthorne tired of the inconvenient location. Herman Melville, a frequent visitor, was especially fond of the view from here of the Stockbridge Bowl, a panorama of meadows edged by mountains, the highest being Mount Greylock. Melville often walked the six miles from his house at Arrowhead to visit Hawthorne with whom at this time he cultivated a rewarding, mutual friendship. In winter, Melville would bring his St. Bernard dog, which the Hawthorne children rode on in the snow as if it were a pony. If Sophia was not at home, Melville would even be allowed to smoke a cigar in the parlor. Remarkably enough, Melville was writing his great novel *Moby Dick* at Arrowhead at the very time Hawthorne was writing *The House of the Seven Gables* at the Red Cottage. The importance of their friendship is shown by Melville's astute critical essay on Hawthorne's *Mosses from an Old Manse;* it praises the author's "great power of blackness . . . that

Calvinistic sense of Innate Depravity and Original Sin." While Hawthorne lived in the Red Cottage, he planned details for his novel *The Blithedale Romance* with the setting of Brook Farm. This idea evolved as a result of Hawthorne's experience in communal living for a short time under the direction of Rev. Ezra Ripley.

The Wayside, Concord

Another house where the Hawthornes lived after the Old Manse and the Lenox Red Cottage was The Wayside on Lexington Road, in Concord. This was the first home Hawthorne actually owned. As a tribute to his Bowdoin College friend Franklin Pierce, Hawthorne wrote a campaign biography of Pierce at The Wayside (1852). This time on the winning side, as if to compensate for the job he lost at the Salem Custom House, Hawthorne was rewarded by President Pierce with an appointment as American consul at Liverpool, England. Now with three children to care for, Hawthorne badly needed a stable income, which his writing could not supply. He accepted the consulship. When he returned to America after five years in England and Europe, he remodeled The Wayside by making additions. His tower study, for example, is reached by a narrow stairway on the second floor. The study has a high desk or shelf so that Hawthorne could stand and write. Because of the study's location, Hawthorne could appreciate the lovely panoramic view.

The House of the Seven Gables, Salem

The House of the Seven Gables is a Salem landmark made famous by Hawthorne's novel of the same name. Along with the Custom House and Hawthorne's Birthplace, Seven Gables is a favorite tourist attraction. The novel was written in the Berkshires, at Lenox, with Herman Melville as a "not too distant neighbor." *Seven Gables* is a family history of pride, selfishness and arrogance redeemed by innocence and love. It was Hawthorne's way of purifying Salem's conscience of its old traditions and sins. And one must understand what Hawthorne meant when he called his novels "romances" — stories in which the imagination and touches of fantasy play tricks with odd scraps of historical incident discovered by Hawthorne in old records, incidents that provoked his interest and creativity.

The Old Man of the Mountains

"The Great Stone Face" (1848) was one of four stories Hawthorne planned for his third collection of tales, to succeed *Twice Told Tales* and *Mosses from an Old Manse*. It was later named *The Snow Image and Other Twice Told Tales*. The book was being planned at the time when Hawthorne's mother died, and just before Hawthorne began his furious pace of writing *The Scarlet Letter*. "The Great Stone Face" is a tale with an Emersonian moral; it expresses the power of an ideal to shape an individual life. Hawthorne was inspired by a natural formation at Franconia Notch, New Hampshire, once worshipped by Indians as the image of the "Great Spirit," and first seen by a white man in 1805. Since Hawthorne's Uncle Samuel owned a stagecoach line, it was possible for the nephew to travel extensively in summers when he was a young man; he went as far west as Detroit on one trip. On such ventures he gathered ideas for writing, and the image of the Old Man of the Mountains observed on one such trip provided the theme for one of Hawthorne's allegorical tales.

Willey House
Crawford's Notch, New Hampshire

The boulder and plaque mark the site of the Willey House at Crawford's Notch in the White Mountains, New Hampshire: to the east is Maine; to the west are the Connecticut River and the Green Mountains. Crawford's Notch is the setting for Nathaniel Hawthorne's tale "The Ambitious Guest." Caused by a terrible flood, a great landslide occurred here on August 28, 1826. The Willey family ran from their house to a supposed place of safety — but all were killed. Ironically, the house itself was untouched because the landslide divided just at this point. In September 1832 Hawthorne wrote to his mother of his journey through the White Mountains. He had just learned that after the 1826 landslide an extra chair was found at the Willey fireside, and from this detail he imagined an "ambitious" guest visiting the family before the catastrophe. The tale that he later wrote grew out of the comments written to his mother; its conflict deals with the lure that leads the traveler on and the known safety of the family hearth.

PATRICK HEMINGWAY
1928 —
Photograph, Kennedy Library

Patrick Hemingway, first son of Ernest and Pauline (Ernest's second wife), was one of the special guests at the dedication of the Hemingway Room of the John F. Kennedy Library, Boston, held July 19, 1980. Also present for this celebration were Madeline Miller, Ernest Hemingway's sister; Charles Scribner, Jr., whose firm published most of Hemingway's books; Jacqueline Onassis; and George Plimpton, whose main address, dealing with anecdote reminiscences of Hemingway, ended with an account of a mock boxing match. Mary Hemingway was at the last moment too ill to attend, but it was through her friendship with Mrs. Onassis and because of her admiration for President Kennedy that this Library became the repository of Hemingway's papers. The prologue to John Kennedy's book *Profiles in Courage* quotes Hemingway's famous phrase "grace under pressure." The Hemingway Library, contains a wealth of author's galleys, notes, poetry, scrapbooks and correspondence. Big game trophies such as an impala head and a lion skin speak to Hemingway's hunting skills, and a large photograph collection recoups his entire life. Patrick Hemingway came from Bozeman, Montana to attend this celebration for his father; before Bozeman, he had lived in East Africa, devoting his time to wildlife protection.

SINCLAIR LEWIS
1885 — 1951
Thorvale Farm

A highly-respected novelist, Sinclair Lewis lived at Thorvale Farm, 4½ miles south of Williamstown, Massachusetts, on Oblong Road. The fine and spacious house is set on 750 acres of field, wood and mountain, commanding from its front terraces a splendid view of Mount Greylock. Lewis bought the estate in 1946 for $45,000 and made repairs and improvements costing $70,000. Although one cottage was used as servants' quarters, there were also a guest cottage, tennis court, and a swimming pool. There were barns, a sugar maple grove of 3,000 trees, and a house for a farmer. While living here, Lewis wrote *Kingsblood Royal* (1947), a study of the persecution of a Negro family in a white neighborhood. Previously, as the leading satirist of his generation, Lewis had written his well-known novels *Main Street*, *Arrowsmith*, *Babbit*, *Cass Timberlane*, *Dodsworth*, and *Elmer Gantry*. At Thorvale Farm he entertained frequently, enjoying the company of Bennett Cerf and Norman Mailer. Lewis is remembered for his vehement crusade against materialism, bigotry, and superficiality.

HENRY WADSWORTH LONGFELLOW
1807 — 1882
Portrait

Called the "national bard" in his day, Longfellow showed his optimism, interest in people, and "love of a good lesson" in his poetry. He was respected and admired by British as well as American readers. A bust of Longfellow is found in the Poets Corner of Westminster Abbey, London. He is buried in Mount Auburn Cemetery, not far from Craigie House, Cambridge, Massachusetts. One of his best-known poems, "The Building of the Ship" (1850) is a tribute to its unnamed real-life hero, James McKay, builder of the greatest clipper ships in the world. Records set by McKay's *Flying Cloud* have never been broken by any other sailing vessel. In the closing of Longfellow's poem, through the symbol of the ship, Longfellow also pleads for union of the nation, a plea which caused Lincoln's eyes to fill with tears when he heard the poem read. During World War II Winston Churchill also quoted part of the poem's closing in an appeal he made for Allied unity.

Longfellow's Wayside Inn

Found in South Sudbury, Massachusetts, off U.S. 20, is the Wayside Inn that Longfellow wrote about after visiting there. Longfellow's engaging innkeeper told such intriguing tales that the poet was encouraged to write about them in his book *Tales of the Wayside Inn* (1863). Everyone recalls the famous first lines, "Listen, my children, and you shall hear/ Of the midnight ride of Paul Revere." Longfellow wrote many such poems that remain in our hearts and thoughts. At the Inn, in the Longfellow Parlor that the poet describes, one finds some of the poet's family mementoes, the famous fireplace, and the piano. The Wayside Inn was restored in the 1930's by a grant from the Ford Foundation. Previously called the Red Horse Tavern, it is used today for overnight guests and for diners. The room in which Longfellow stayed is typical of rural 18th century accommodations. It has a pencil post bed, Spanish foot chairs, and a highboy — prized examples of colonial furniture. Close by is the Lafayette bedroom. On the glass near one of the downstairs doorways is the name "Molyneux," which is featured in one of the best tales of Nathaniel Hawthorne, "My Kinsman, Major Molineux."

Craigie House

Henry Wadsworth Longfellow was born in Portland, Maine, February 27, 1807. A romantic, he is admired for his narrative poems. From 1837-1882 he lived in Craigie House, 105 Brattle Street, Cambridge, Massachusetts. The house was a wedding gift from Longfellow's father-in-law. During the American Revolution, this dwelling served as George Washington's headquarters; in fact, Washington's dining room was later used as Longfellow's study. Here Longfellow entertained writer friends such as William Dean Howells, Ralph Waldo Emerson, Nathaniel Hawthorne, Richard Henry Dana, and James Russell Lowell. The British writer Charles Dickens visited here too. Many of Longfellow's famous poems were written in his study at the upright desk where he composed the narrative poem *Evangeline.* Toward the back of the house was his library with more than 10,000 books; this was also the music room and ballroom. The room had paintings used by Longfellow in *The Song of Hiawatha.* One of his more familiar poems, "The Children's Hour," describes Longfellow's daughters descending the front stairway: "Grave Alice and laughing Allegra, and Edith with golden hair." While Longfellow and his family lived in Craigie House (named for Longfellow's predecessor), he taught languages and literature at Harvard. A Longfellow Memorial, his statue, is found in Brattle Street, Cambridge. A literary memorial is the title of Robert Frost's first book of poems *A Boy's Will*, which comes from the refrain of Longfellow's poem "My Lost Youth."

Longfellow's Arm-Chair

On Longfellow's seventy-second birthday the children of Cambridge presented him with a chair made from wood of the "spreading chestnut tree" celebrated in Longfellow's poem "The Village Blacksmith." When Brattle Street was widened, this tree was cut down. On the location of the smithy is a fine Cambridge restaurant. The arm-chair is still to be seen at Craigie House.

JAMES RUSSELL LOWELL
1819 — 1891
Elmwood

Elmwood, James Russell Lowell's home, is at the corner of Mt. Auburn and Elmwood Streets, Cambridge, Massachusetts. Lowell, a poet, critic, editor and Harvard professor, loved to entertain and teach his students in his study as he sat by a fireplace and smoked his pipe. His good friends, poets Henry Wadsworth Longfellow and Oliver Wendell Holmes, visited with him frequently. Lowell was very much interested in politics, and he expressed his opposition to the Mexican War in *The Biglow Papers*, which were very popular because they were amusingly written in a Yankee dialect. His long poem *A Fable for Critics* analyzes other contemporary writers, and his masterpiece "The Vision of Sir Launfal" speaks of the Holy Grail. Lowell became American ambassador to Great Britain and enjoyed his status as a cultural representative. He is buried in Mt. Auburn Cemetery close to Elmwood, a place whose beauty he had always admired. Poets Amy Lowell and Robert Lowell are descendants of James Russell Lowell.

HERMAN MELVILLE

1819 — 1891

Seamen's Bethel, New Bedford, Massachusetts

Seamen's Bethel is found on Johnny Cake Hill, Exit 22 on I-95, New Bedford, Massachusetts. Before entering, one sees a plaque that quotes Herman Melville's words about the chapel. There are two floors: the lower one has wooden benches and a plain altar for sailors to come in and worship informally; the second floor is more formal in that it looks like a New England church. During the heyday of whaling, as many as 5,000 sailors could be found at any one time in the New Bedford port. Having visited the Bethel many times, Melville describes the chapel in his novel *Moby Dick*.

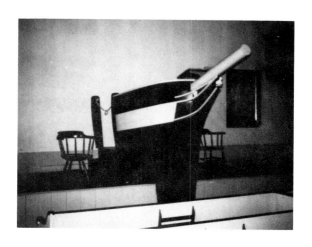

Seamen's Bethel Pulpit

In Melville's great novel *Moby Dick* a minister called Father Mapple (in real life, Enoch Mudge) preaches from a pulpit that is shaped like the prow of a ship. And a mighty sermon it is, on the text of Jonah and the whale! The front of the pulpit is paneled, and the Bible sits on a carved piece of wood resembling the beak of a ship. Melville further described the pulpit as having a rope ladder, which Father Mapple used to ascend to his place; in reality, no rope ladder existed. Around the walls of the Seamen's Bethel are small marble plaques in memory of New Bedford men who died at sea. Melville makes no mention of these in *Moby Dick;* the attention of Ishmael, narrator of the novel, is fixed on the pulpit and the preacher. But had he noticed these somber memorials, he would have found an ill omen prophetic of the fate of the *Pequod,* the whaling vessel he is about to serve on; after it is destroyed by the great white whale, he is the only survivor. Melville does refer in this early chapter of his novel to a foot-powered organ; it is still there in the Seamen's Bethel. In real life, but not in the novel, Mudge on one occasion took the organ by wheelbarrow to the New Bedford docks so that the sailors who were shipping out would experience a complete religious service.

In 1850 Melville and his family moved from New York to Arrowhead, a farm located at 780 Holmes Road, Pittsfield, Massachusetts. At one time, this white frame house was owned by another family member. Melville planned to raise potatoes and corn as a part-time husbandman, with the rest of his time devoted to writing. In the back of the house is a long, wooden porch Melville built called the "Piazza"; he thought it resembled the deck of a ship. Here he wrote *The Piazza Tales* with their settings in the Berkshires. His study, now called the Moby Dick Room located on the second floor, faced Mount Greylock in the Berkshire Mountains, about twenty miles away. This seafaring writer thought that Mount Greylock looked like a whale surfacing. Little wonder that he wrote his greatest novel *Moby Dick*, the first literary classic of whaling, at Arrowhead. Since his readers were expecting more adventure tales like *Typee* and *Omoo*, they were disappointed in *Moby Dick*, and it was not an immediate success. But later, encouraged by Sophia Hawthorne, Melville wrote *Pierre*, a strange, disguised amalgam of his own personal frustrations, and because of financial difficulties he sold his beloved Arrowhead to his brother Allan in 1863. When Melville was still living at Arrowhead, Nathaniel Hawthorne lived six miles away at Lenox. This was a perfect relationship for the two writers, who became close friends, and who influenced each other's books; in fact, Melville dedicated *Moby Dick* to Hawthorne.

EDWIN ARLINGTON ROBINSON
1869 — 1935
Home in Gardiner, Maine

As one drives up a long hill from the town below in Gardiner, Maine, he is reminded of Robinson's poem "Mr. Flood's Party." In the poem, Eben Flood climbed the hill from Tilbury Town (Robinson's name for Gardiner) and held a lonely one-man party. Sadly enough, his former town friends were gone. Edwin Arlington Robinson lived in a white frame house with spacious grounds at the top of the hill at 67 Lincoln Avenue. The house is located on a corner in a residential area. Robinson loved this house where he was reared with his two brothers, and he lived there until 1896. He wrote about the townspeople of Gardiner, giving them odd, fictitious names such as Cliff Klingenhagen, Richard Cory and Luke Havergal. Unfortunately, his characters all had problems too difficult to overcome, ones that were reminiscent of Robinson's own many problems. President Theodore Roosevelt helped Robinson out of financial straits in 1905 by appointing him as customs inspector in New York, but Robinson's troubles persisted even though he had additional help from friends. In 1911, Robinson was subsidized and lionized at the McDowell Colony, New Hampshire, a setting which he enjoyed. He did most of his writing at the Colony during the summers, and he returned to New York City in winter.

51

E. A. Robinson Monument

Edwin Arlington Robinson, philosophical poet who turned to writing long narratives in later years, was cremated and buried in the family plot about a block from the Robinson home in Gardiner, Maine. A memorial plaque for the poet is found in a small park also located about two blocks from the Robinson House.

HENRY DAVID THOREAU
1817 — 1862
Portrait

Owned by the Concord Antiquarian Society, the portrait of Thoreau was painted in 1839. It is difficult to believe that this shy person would sit long enough to have a portrait done. Although he enjoyed his two years of solitude at Walden Pond, he did not isolate himself there. In fact, he walked to town frequently to visit and to secure supplies. He and his close friend Ralph Waldo Emerson often spent many hours together. Emerson loved to visit Walden Pond, which was very near his home, and he frequently sat on a rock near the cabin and meditated. He and Thoreau were such close friends that many people commented that they looked alike. It was also said that a listener had difficulty in distinguishing between the voices of the two men when they conversed in another room.

Cabin at Walden Pond

Within the Walden Pond State Reservation is the site where Thoreau erected a cabin in 1845 on Emerson's land. Today, a replica of the cabin is found behind the Concord Lyceum. Near the cabin's original location is a plaque with a famous quotation from his chapter from *Walden* "Where I Lived and What I Lived For": "I went to the woods to live completely, to front the essential facts of life." Thoreau built the cabin with borrowed or cheaply bought material, ten by fifteen feet in size. He also built his own furniture. In a nearby field he planted potatoes, beans, corn and other vegetables which he sold after keeping a share for himself. Loving to commune with nature, he was able to tell exactly when a particular wild flower would open. Thoreau's *Walden, or Life in the Woods* (1854) remains one of the best nature books in American literature, which is to say that it is a book about man's harmonious relationship with nature. Thoreau said that three chairs were sufficient for him in his cabin — one for solitude, two for friendship, and three for company. When he was visited by more than two guests, the others would have to stand.

Thoreau's Lyceum can be seen at 156 Belknap Street, Concord, Massachusetts. Here there are some belongings that exemplify Thoreau's simple style of living: his desk, surveying maps, and other artifacts. Thoreau had many interests, and some thought that he drifted from one to another too easily. His family had a pencil factory, and he designed an efficient lead pencil which he nevertheless refused to produce in quantities because he did not care to repeat himself in an enterprise. He lived in his cabin at Walden Pond for two years and a few months; but, when he discovered that he had worn a path to the cabin door, he decided that he was becoming a creature of habit and that it was time to turn to other interests. At intervals he taught school, but also he was a qualified land surveyor, a fine classical scholar, and one of the greatest of American naturalists. Both Emerson and Thoreau were lecturers at the original Lyceum; in fact, Thoreau served as its secretary.

Site of the Old Jail, Concord

Henry David Thoreau was imprisoned for one night in jail on this site in July 1846 for refusing to recognize the right of the state of Massachusetts to collect a nine shilling tax. In particular, Thoreau was protesting against the Fugitive Slave Act. The prison episode has been made famous by his essay "Civil Disobedience." This and other works of Thoreau inspired Ghandi with the concept of passive resistance in Ghandi's efforts to win freedom for India from British rule; and in turn, the American Civil Rights Movement as led by Dr. Martin Luther King, Jr., also employed Ghandi's strategy of peaceful protest against unjust laws. The Concord Old Jail marker is found where the jail once stood, on the southwest corner of Monument Square in the center of Concord. While Henry was in jail, his friend Ralph Waldo Emerson went to see him and asked what Henry was "doing in there." In turn, Henry asked what his friend was doing "out there." His quip to Emerson expressed his strong commitments, and it implied that Emerson was not doing enough to defend the cause of justice. But part of Thoreau's style was that of being or seeming to be a casual, understated person. Thus when he was arrested, he was on his way to the cobbler's (as he says in "Civil Disobedience"), and upon his release he went huckleberrying. Tradition has it that a relative paid the fine for his release in order to avoid scandal, but he made little of this gesture, remarking instead that he enjoyed visiting with the other inmates while he was in jail.

Henry David Thoreau's grave is located on Authors Ridge, Sleepy Hollow Cemetery, on Bedford Street, State Route 62, Concord. He would have approved of his eight by seven inch gravestone because of its simplicity and the one word "Henry" on it. Other members of his family are buried with him in the family plot. At the time of Thoreau's death, since he left no money for burial, his friends collected money to pay for the simple monument. The Hawthorne, Emerson and Alcott families are buried nearby, just as they were near neighbors during their lifetimes.

MARK TWAIN
1835 — 1910
Mark Twain House, Hartford

Located at 351 Farmington Avenue, Hartford, Connecticut, "The Mark Twain Memorial" is in the area called Nook Farm where Twain lived 1874-1901. Being a licensed riverboat pilot, Twain wanted riverboat features in the house. This "steamboat Gothic" structure has its original Italian marble floors, a Venetian bed with an angel on each bedpost, a Steinway grand piano which Twain played by ear, walls hand-stenciled by Tiffany, and chandeliers and windows furnished by Tiffany. Twain had the first telephone in Hartford. On the third floor is a large billiard room where he did much of his writing and played billiards every Friday evening with friends such as Irving, Howells and Aldrich. Others attended his many dinner parties. While he lived here he wrote *A Connecticut Yankee in King Arthur's Court*, *A Tramp Abroad*, *Life on the Mississippi*, *The Prince and the Pauper*, and *The Adventures of Huckleberry Finn*. His desk faced away from the window to avoid distraction, a window he had made of marble carved in such a way as to angle the light over his writing desk. About this curious mansion he composed a humorous poem that begins, "This is the house that Mark built."

In the billiard room of the Mark Twain House in Hartford hangs Twain's famous crimson academic gown, hood, and cap presented to the author by Oxford University. When Twain re-

ceived a cablegram in 1907 from Oxford to go to England to receive an honorary degree, he was flattered, and he decided to make the trip in spite of his ill health. He had already received two honorary degrees — one from Yale and one from Missouri, but to receive a Doctor of Letters degree from prestigious Oxford was a special honor. In *The Autobiography of Mark Twain* edited by Charles Neider, Twain jokingly tells how much he deserved to receive this distinction. He was so pleased with it that he even wore the cap, gown, and hood to his eldest daughter Clara's wedding when she married the pianist Ossip Gabrilowitsch. One of the earliest examples of color photography, recently reproduced in *The National Geographic Magazine*, is of Mark Twain wearing the famous crimson robe.

EDITH WHARTON
1862 — 1937
The Mount

From 1904-1913 novelist Edith Wharton lived in the stately mansion she called "Mount" located near Lenox, Massachusetts. In her autobiography *A Backward Glance*, she refers to it as spacious and dignified. It is a copy of an early Georgian Manor in Lincoln-shire, England with a cupola and walkway on top. Wharton wrote her well-known novel *Ethan Frome* (with its Lenox setting) while she lived at the Mount. Among the many friends who visited her here were Theodore Roosevelt, then President of the United States; Henry Cabot Lodge; and the novelist Henry James, who wrote about his stimulating experiences at the Mount. In *The American Scene* he describes the autumnal landscape which charmed him, and he speculates on the rise of an American leisure class which seems to him a good omen. Wharton's novels, such as *The House of Mirth*, deal with the moneyed, leisure class of "old" New York to which Wharton herself belonged. The Mount had a huge courtyard and many piazzas looking out to formal gardens. It also resembled an Italian villa with its marble floors and fireplaces and its ela-borately decorated rooms. One of Wharton's books is about her special interest in interior decorating. To this day the carved mouldings can be seen in all the rooms of the Mount. For many years after it was sold by Wharton, it was used by the Foxhollow School for Girls.

JOHN GREENLEAF WHITTIER
1807 — 1892
Whittier Homestead

The Haverhill, Massachusetts, homestead of the poet John Greenleaf Whittier's family was chosen in 1688 by Thomas Whittier because it was near the Quaker Meeting House. The farmhouse remains much as it was when Whittier lived there from 1807-1836.

After hearing the poetry of Robert Burns, which appealed to ordinary people, he was influenced to write similar works on the humble pleasures of labor. He attended Haverhill Academy for six years and later became an outstanding editor. His poetry deals with antislavery, events in New England's early history, Indian legends, the simplicity of rural New England, and religious doubts and beliefs. With his dedication to antislavery, he constantly urged fellow-writers Longfellow, Lowell and Emerson to become abolitionists and was very influential in helping John Quincy Adams' antislavery campaign. Showing a romantic phase of America's past, Whittier's poem "The Barefoot Boy" describes a boy sitting on the backdoor step of the Haverhill house as he eats his milk and bread. The barn across the road from the farmhouse is the one the boys tunneled to in Whittier's poem *Snow Bound*.

Hearth at the Haverhill Home

The hearth of the Whittier homestead has features described in Whittier's masterpiece *Snow Bound*. He associates the blaze of the fire with the reality of family love, and he unites the family with the warmth from the hearth. The members of the Whittier clan are "Shut in from all the world without" during the snow storm. The poem records, "While the red logs before us beat/ The frost-line back with tropic heat." Members of the family in the poem relate tales and anecdotes for their mutual entertainment while the blizzard rages outside.

The Haverhill homestead was sold in 1836, the Whittiers moved to Amesbury, and they purchased a house on Friend Street to be near the Quaker Meeting House, since the family were devout followers. Whittier was a bachelor who devoted his slender income to his family; he spent over forty years writing in this house. The house remains much as it was while he lived there, during which time he published twelve volumes of poetry and continued as crusading editor in the antislavery cause. His seventieth birthday was celebrated at a famous dinner given in his honor by the *Atlantic Monthly* and attended by every outstanding American writer of the day. The decorum of this Eastern Establishment occasion was upset by a brash young Westerner named Mark Twain, who in his birthday speech for Whittier had three drunken derelicts from the West impersonate Longfellow, Emerson, and Holmes. Like Queen Victoria, the Easterners were not amused. Whittier survived the event, however, and his eightieth birthday was celebrated nationally for his dedication to the simple American life.

EAST

PEARL S. BUCK
1892 — 1973
Portrait

Famed Nobel Prize winner and author Pearl Buck, who was born in Hillsboro, West Virginia, spent her early years in China as the daughter of American missionaries. From her experiences in the Orient she was able to write many well-known novels, including *The Good Earth*, a 1932 Pulitzer Prize winner. Some of her best-known works are: *China As I See It*, *The Kennedy Women*, *China Past and Present* and *The Goddess Abides*. Of her many novels, she gave her own name to those with an Oriental setting; and she gave the name of John Sedges, her *nom de plume*, to those with an American setting. Three Sedges' books are *The Townsman*, *The Long Love* and *Voices in the House*. Buck's novel *A Bridge for Passing* uses poetic-prose to paint a word-picture of the new Japan to which she returned after a twenty-five years' absence. While she was in Japan, she received word of the death of her husband, New York publisher Richard J. Walsh, and she described her sense of loss hauntingly in *A Bridge for Passing*. Her *Words of Love* appeared posthumously in 1974.

Green Hills Farm
Perkasie, Bucks County, Pennsylvania

Pearl Buck spent the second half of her life at Green Hills Farm, bought in 1934. Both Oriental and American interests are observed in the decor of the house. Among these are a Pennsylvania Dutch hutch, a small organ, colorful Chinese rugs, and Oriental wall hangings located in a living room on the first floor. Her bedroom on the second floor contains her important writing desk where she wrote many of her more than 100 books. Another room on the second floor contains many of her awards and honors. Of exceptional note is the International Headquarters of the Pearl S. Buck Foundation located at Green Hills Farms. As a youth in Shanghai, Buck became aware of slave girls who had run away from owners, and she did small chores in a home for the poor, mostly prostitutes. Even after she married her first husband, John Lossing Buck, an agricultural expert, they lived in northern China where she observed the slaving peasants. These social injustices led her to organize the Foundation which also offers help for Amerasian offspring. Here is a writer who spent her life bringing the East and West together in her novels and in her philanthropic deeds. She reared nine adopted children, four of them after the death of her second husband. An excellent novelist, true humanitarian and noted teacher, Pearl Buck is buried at Green Hills Farm in a small grove of trees near the main road.

WILLA CATHER

1873 — 1947
Allegheny High School, Pittsburgh

In 1901 Willa Cather accepted a teaching position in Pittsburgh's Central High School, located at the corner of Bedford Avenue and Fulton Street. She transferred to Allegheny High School, Arch

Street, North Side in 1903. Her beginning salary was $650 a year and was increased to $1,300 by 1906 when she left. Her enjoyment and dedication to teaching were shown by her working with many students after hours in small groups and by her reading exemplary themes aloud in class. Through such efforts, the students were encouraged with their creative writing. She was very popular and the students loved her. Besides teaching, Cather spent much time at the Carnegie Library, Museum and Music Hall. A music critic, she attended many concerts where she met and visited with her students as well as with city dignitaries. But at the same time she was doing her own writing. Her book of poems *April Twilights* was successfully published in 1903. She also published several short stories with settings in the Pittsburgh area. Best known are "Paul's Case," which describes the Schenley Hotel and Carnegie Music Hall, Oakland; "A Gold Slipper," Oakland and East Liberty; "Double Birthday," North Side, Pittsburgh where Cather taught; and "Uncle Valentine," nearby Edgeworth, where Cather visited with her dear friends the Ethelbert Nevins. The Nevin estate, called Vineacre, was located on Woodland Road, Edgeworth. On Sundays, Willa would come by train to Edgeworth, then walk uphill to the Nevin home to enjoy the atmosphere created by charming pianist and composer, Ethelbert Nevin, and his family.

McClung Home, Pittsburgh

Willa Cather lived at the home of Judge Samuel Alfred McClung and his daughter Isabelle from 1901-1906. The address was 1180 Murray Hill Avenue; the street is still paved with its original Belgian block stone. Cather had arrived in Pittsburgh in 1896 to be managing editor of *Home Monthly*, whose policy she said in its opening number was "to entertain, to educate, to elevate." She did not find her task very rewarding, and the next year she was working for the *Pittsburgh Leader*, a job which she continued until 1901, when she turned to teaching. As critic for the *Leader*, she met Lizzie Hudson Collier, an actress very popular at this time; but it was Lizzie who in 1899 introduced Willa to her friend Isabelle McClung, who was in Pittsburgh's *Social Register*. Because of their interest in the arts, Isabelle and Willa became friends immediately and enduringly. Willa had tried and disliked four boarding houses in Pittsburgh, so she was pleased to join the prestigious McClung family in their home on Murray Hill Avenue. Isabelle enjoyed the stimulation of Willa's active life, and they complemented one another. In 1902 they toured Europe together. While living in the McClung home for five years, Willa was not a boarder; she was a guest who was not permitted to pay her way. Willa was especially happy to be near the home of her friends Dr. and Mrs. Lawrence Litchfield, located at 5431 Fifth Avenue and Elizabeth Moorhead Vermorcken. After the death of Judge McClung, his house was sold in 1915-1916. By 1903, Willa already had come to the attention of S. S. McClure through his acceptance of two of her best short stories for his magazine, and it was McClure who invited her to edit that magazine in New York in 1906.

JAMES FENIMORE COOPER

1789 — 1851

Episcopal Church, Cooperstown, New York

Cooperstown, New York, is known to almost every American for its Baseball Hall of Fame, but its name comes from the family of James Fenimore Cooper, among the earliest and most popular of American novelists. He lived in Otsego Hall, the family mansion overlooking Lake Otsego (called Glimmerglass in the novels), and he borrowed the lifestyle of an English country gentleman. But Cooper especially loved the outdoor life of the then-frontier of western New York State. His greatest, most inventive creation is a frontier hero variously called Leatherstocking, Natty Bumpo, or Hawkeye whose remarkable feats of hunting, marksmanship and bravery rival the skills of any Indian. Even though Mark Twain ridiculed Cooper's Indians for being as wooden as cigar store Indians, Cooper's *Leatherstocking Tales* have had universal appeal: English, French and Russian readers have found these works to be vastly entertaining. Cooper and his wife were married in the Episcopal Church in Cooperstown, and they are buried in the Church cemetery. Close by is a fine bronze statue of Cooper, and scattered about the shores of Lake Otsego are markers citing points of interest that can be identified with scenes from Cooper's novels.

EMILY DICKINSON
1830 — 1886
Arch Street Presbyterian Church, Philadelphia

Only twice during her lifetime was Emily Dickinson away from her home in Amherst, Massachusetts — once in Washington, D.C., in connection with her father's duties there as congressman; and once in Philadelphia, where she heard the Rev. Charles Wadsworth preach at the Arch Street Presbyterian Church. Inferences drawn from her poetry by some critics maintain that she was in love with him: "If you were coming in the fall/ I'd pass the summer by." The Rev. Wadsworth did visit her at her home in Amherst; but when he was called to serve a congregation in California, it was as if God had once again taken from Emily a special, devoted friend: "I never lost as much but twice." Her poems, whose rhythms are odd variations of old New England hymns, are now judged as the greatest work of any American woman writer. They are probably autobiographical in some sense, but with secretive, oblique references to the poet's joys, self-denials, and frustrations.

F. SCOTT FITZGERALD
1896 — 1940
Great Neck, Long Island

It was F. Scott Fitzgerald who named the Jazz Age that he depicted so brilliantly in his novels. Emancipated, disillusioned and cynical, his characters love high living and spending which eventually lead to tragedy and failure. Fitzgerald, a mid-westerner, was born in St. Paul, Minnesota, but the family lived in several different houses there. When he left home to attend Princeton, he returned to St. Paul infrequently. Interested in writing even as a youth, he produced acceptable short stories before he was seventeen years old. He was fascinated by and emulated the lifestyle of the very rich; his best novel *The Great Gatsby* analyzes that style of living and its fatal effects on the hero. Scott and Zelda, his beautiful, temperamental wife, themselves set a comparably fast pace of living in New York: for their disorderly behavior they were asked to leave the Biltmore Hotel while staying there during their honeymoon. Moving to the Commodore, they aroused further notice when Zelda took her famous swims in the fountain across the street. Zelda preferred flesh-colored bathing suits. Their favorite New York hotel, however, was the Plaza. The estate where they lived at great expense on Long Island was at Great Neck; that flavor is caught in *Gatsby* with the estates of Jay Gatsby and Tom and Daisy Buchanan. Paris, the Riviera, and Palm Beach were other expensive haunts of the Fitzgeralds until Zelda had to spend increasingly long stays in sanitariums, and Scott too was hospitalized for alcoholism. Like Faulkner, Fitzgerald worked as a Hollywood script writer, but unlike Faulkner he was also exceedingly well-paid for his novels and stories. Nevertheless, Scott and Zelda's style of living more than exhausted his earning powers. Fitzgerald's *The Last Tycoon*, incomplete and posthumously published, fictionalizes some of the meteoric glamor of the boy-wonder Hollywood movie producer Irving Thalberg in the character of Monroe Stahr. The enormous talent of Stahr/Thalberg and the fact that it is doomed to die early, is symptomatic of Fitzgerald's own power, brilliant and burned out early. As a prose stylist, Fitzgerald is almost a poet; he has often been called the poet of the Jazz Age.

BENJAMIN FRANKLIN
1706 — 1790
Boston and Philadelphia

The prototype for the American achiever, the fulfillment of our myth, the American Dream, Benjamin Franklin was an extraordinarily complex person even though his simple message to Americans may seem like a truism. Like all great myths, it is an ideal the culture accepts; like our constitutional right to happiness, we pursue it. Its tangible nature is as varied as the character and achievements of Franklin himself. The common denominator of all those achievements is the principle of the "self-made" person, who Franklin was in a very real and singular sense. As typesetter and journalist in Boston, he quickly learned to evade the physical discipline of the older brother he was apprenticed to; and when the brother was jailed by censorship-prone authorities, Ben quickly learned to be editor and to avoid legal complications for himself. He even bargained, cleverly, with the brother to release him from that apprenticeship in return for being editor during the brother's incarceration. Ben also managed to become an author by carefully imitating the merits of writers he liked, and made his unwitting editor-brother his publisher. Herman Melville disliked Franklin's philosophy and methods of achieving his goals; and he satirized Franklin in his novel *Israel Potter*. Yet if Franklin's pragmatic way in life is shrewd (perhaps even self-serving), it took advantage of others only when they were dishonest or incompetent; or at the very least he learned good personal lessons in how to avoid such misconduct. Philosopher, educator, writer and editor, statesman, inventor and scientist — Franklin's many roles in an array of great skills and disciplines enriched the struggling colonies and enabled them to move toward true statehood. At the closing of Fitzgerald's *The Great Gatsby*, Jay's father finds among his dead son's effects a small record book done in the manner of Franklin's scheduled plan for self-improvement. More mundane, but still a part of the American Dream, are the Horatio Alger books that buoyed the hopes of many an ambitious, but poor, American youth of the 19th century. Franklin's *Autobiography* is one book that belongs in any collection of Americana, regardless of how small. The original manuscript (with one ink-spilled page scholars have never been able to decipher) is now in one of the great libraries of the world — the Huntington Library at San Marino, California. It may be said that Franklin had two beginnings: on Milk Street, Boston, where he was born the tenth of fifteen children; and on Market Street, Philadelphia, where at age seventeen he walked along, almost penniless, munching a puffy roll.

SAMUEL J. HAZO
1928 —
Carnegie Lecture Hall, Pittsburgh

Born in Bloomfield, Pittsburgh, Dr. Samuel Hazo was graduated from Notre Dame, Duquesne University, and the University of Pittsburgh. A well-known poet, some of his books include *Discovery and Other Poems* (1959), *The Quiet War* (1962), *My Sons in God*, *Once for the Last Bandit* (1972), *Quartered* (1974), *To Paris* (1981), *Thank a Bored Angel* (1983). His most recent novel is *The Wanton Summer Air* (1982). He is a prolific writer who portrays various aspects of his life as a traveler, army lieutenant, family man, university professor, and writer. "There's more to certitude/ than sound or sight./ There's/ more than darkness to the night." Thus, as he would say, poetry makes palpable that which is at first only conceptual: in a modern way, he does what the metaphysical poets did — to create unlikely combinations of things that give us a whole new view of life. Hazo is a Professor of English at Duquesne University. Besides writing poetry, he has published translations and criticisms. As Director of the International Poetry Forum, he has brought many outstanding writers and performers to Pittsburgh for the Forum at Carnegie Lecture Hall: W. H. Auden, Julie Harris in the persona of Emily Dickinson, Princess Grace of Monaco speaking Shakespeare, and others.

WASHINGTON IRVING
1783 — 1859
Portrait

Washington Irving, handsome, charming, and gregarious, was the first outstanding American romanticist. Well-liked in America and Europe, his urbanity is easily recognized in the extravagant American humor found in *The Sketch Book* and in *A History of New York* by "Diedrich Knickerbocker," a satirical burlesque. Irving's influence at home and abroad soon earned him the position of diplomat to Spain 1826-1829. He became an expert in Spanish history. Later he served as minister to Spain, 1842-1845. But because of an extension of his family business in Birmingham and the settling of his sister Sarah and her husband Henry Van Wart in that city, he became attached to England and served as Secretary of the American Legation in London (1829-1831). He spent the last years of his life in America suffering from severe attacks of asthma. Nevertheless, although many visitors came to see him, he could never turn anyone away.

The entrance to Washington Irving's estate of Sunnyside features bronze castings representing two of Irving's most famous characters, which flank a bust of Irving himself. The figure on the left is of Rip Van Winkle, bemused after his twenty-year nap by the changes wrought in his village after the American Revolution.

The comic tale about him makes Rip the victim of a nagging wife who, during Rip's absence, is said to have died of a stroke brought on by arguing with a New England peddler. In Dame Van Winkle's death Irving also mirrors the release of the colonies from the nagging "mother" country, England. Amusingly, at his homecoming Rip says he is a loyal subject of the King, whereupon the town folk threaten him as a despised Tory. In this tale, as in others, Irving pokes fun at the sleepiness of the Dutch settlers who let time pass them by. The other figure at the Sunnyside Entrance is Boabdil, last of the Moorish kings of Granada. According to the legend related in one of Irving's *Tales of the Alhambra* (1832), Boabdil and his armies were not driven out of Spain, but were enclosed in a mountain by magic. Once a year, on the Eve of St. John (the anniversary of Boabdil's defeat), followers of Allah are allowed to come and pay homage to their king. When the spell is broken, Boabdil and his troops will once again come down from their mountain and reclaim the throne in the Alhambra and the kingdom of Granada. In 1829, in addition to writing a book about

Columbus while he was in Spain, Irving traveled by mule to the Alhambra Castle and lived there a short time in one of the many deserted rooms. The Alhambra is really a series of Moorish palaces and towers with heavy fortifications surrounding them. Its history begins even before the 9th century, and ends only with the 15th (1492), when Christian armies seized it from the Moors. Thus Irving's romantic affinity for the past is expressed by the two figures at the Entrance to Sunnyside.

Sunnyside

Tarrytown, New York is the lovely setting for Washington Irving's twenty-acre estate called Sunnyside. In 1818, the town overlooked a stream of traffic going up the Hudson River to supply materials to dig the Erie Canal. River and Canal were to become the great highway to the frontier, and yet a pastoral tone is still found in the area. Sunnyside sits beside the great River immortalized not only by Irving but also by such painters as Thomas Cole, Durand and Kensett; in fact, about fifty artists belong to the so-called Hudson Valley Group. During Irving's years at Sunnyside the picturesque estate became a favorite gathering place for leading world figures who flocked about Irving as a tribute to his fame. Originally, Sunnyside was a small stone Dutch cottage (which Irving gradually enlarged), a cove at the end of a quiet lane within strolling distance of the Old Dutch Church at Sleepy Hollow. The bees and ivy were brought here by Irving from Sir Walter Scott's home at Abbotsford, and a small lake close to the house was named "Little Mediterranean." Irving describes Sunnyside as "a little old-fashioned stone mansion, all made up of gable ends, and as full of angles and corners as an old cocked hat."

Sunnyside, Study

Irving's study, the first room to the right on the ground floor, contains his personal book collection. The desk, given to him by his publisher, G. P. Putnam, is covered with several of Irving's personal effects, but it was used for his many hours of writing. At the back of the room, in front of a bookcase, is a sofa where Irving could rest. He would soften the noises and secure his privacy from his brother and two nieces by drawing the drapes before the sofa. Eventually, because of the noise resulting from the railroad built along the Hudson River, Irving gave up his second floor bedroom, which was on the river side, and used the study as a bedroom. A large leather chair was apparently used by Irving and his many visitors since he loved to entertain them in his study, even though they interrupted him from his writing. The most monumental of his efforts is a five-volume biography of George Washington, the last portion of which was finished only a short time before Irving's death.

Plaque, Christ Church (Episcopal), Tarrytown

CHRIST CHURCH
Erected in 1871, for many
Years Washington Irving
Was vestryman and warden
Ivy is from cuttings from
Vine on his home Sunnyside

Located on the corner of South Broadway and Elizabeth Streets in Tarrytown, Christ Church with its pointed windows and arches reflects Irving's interest in Moorish architecture. In the Church, the old marble altar seems to be stained and therefore has been covered with wood grain. A separate pew on the right bears Irving's name. There is also a bust of Irving. In a room behind the pulpit is a cabinet containing a silver communion service given to the Church by Irving. These pieces are used twice a year. It is said that Irving was a devout churchman, communicant and warden. He almost always took the offering when he attended church — an act which all parishoners and guests looked forward to. The original Church record book still remains that names Irving as a communicant. In 1938, Washington Du Pont Irving, great grand nephew of Washington Irving, replanted a sprig of ivy next to the wall of the Church because the original piece taken from Sunnyside had been removed when the Church was renovated.

82

The Headless Horseman Marker, Tarrytown

The Headless Horseman marker identifies a supposed scene of Tarrytown in Washington Irving's story "The Legend of Sleepy Hollow." In the story, Ichabod Crane, a superstitious schoolmaster who has been courting the country heiress Katrina Van Tassel, is the victim of a practical joke by Brom Bones, a rival for Katrina's affections. According to legend, the ghost of a Hessian soldier haunted the Hollow looking for his head, which had been shot off by a cannon ball in the American Revolution. Brom Bones, masquerading as the ghostly Hessian, pursues Ichabod late at night and throws his "head" at the frightened schoolmaster, who hurriedly leaves Sleepy Hollow. The next day, a smashed pumpkin is revealed to be the "head" thrown at Ichabod. The Old Dutch Church is also near the site of the bridge; Irving is buried in the Church graveyard, supposedly also the "resting" place of the uneasy Hessian.

Irving's Grave

Located in the cemetery of the Old Dutch Church in Tarrytown, the gravestone reads, "Washington Irving, born April 3, 1783, died November 28, 1859." The youngest in a family of eleven children,

Irving was even at thirty the subject of care and attention from his older brothers. He returned their concern by his strong family loyalty. Showing signs of tuberculosis at age twenty-one, Irving was sent on a two-year convalescent tour of Europe by his brothers. Upon returning, he studied law under Judge Josiah Hoffman, but he also began writing skillful parodies of antiquarian histories of New York. Engaged to marry Matilda, Judge Hoffman's daughter, Irving was overcome with grief at her sudden death, and he remained a bachelor for life.

HENRY JAMES
1843 — 1916
Washington Square, New York

A writer's writer, Henry James has won praise from authors as different as Ernest Hemingway and T. S. Eliot. He was also the first international American writer, more profoundly so than his successors, the expatriates of post World War I (Stein, Fitzgerald, Hemingway and others), and he remained (unlike Ezra Pound) distinctively American in sympathies and understanding. The fact that he became a British subject very late in life was simply his way of saying that America should have joined its allies sooner than it did in opposing Germany in the First War. Born in New York City when it still had an almost town atmosphere, James was educated in a variety of schools in both the Old and New worlds. *The Portrait of a Lady* (1881) is the high point of the earliest part of his career, devoted to the "international" theme — what happens to Americans in Europe, and to Europeans in America. Searching for new subjects in mid-career, James turned to social and political themes, to the theater (ill-advisedly), to novellas about artists, and to psychological studies of exploited children and harassed adults. The "major phase" (and the last) again turns to cosmopolitan themes with novels written in a highly convoluted style. James was also a remarkable literary critic, of his own and of others' works. His fiction, especially the later works, is not easily read, but it cannot be ignored or discounted. If any one author transformed the novel from the old 19th century Dickens-Thackery plan of mere storytelling to the modern scheme of psychological analysis, and of workmanlike ways of shaping and moulding the novel into a more controlled and disciplined form than the "loose baggy monsters" of 19th century English fiction, it was Henry James. His Daisy Miller is a worthy predecessor of Fitzgerald's Daisy Buchanan, and his Isabel Archer ranks high among American literary heroines, along with Hawthorne's Hester Prynne. Whereas most important American novelists are chary, even almost squeamish with their women characters, James understood the converse of men and women and expressed it with rich subtlety and understanding. James's frequent childhood visits to his grandmother's house at 19 Washington Square (no longer standing) gave him the sense of place for his novel *Washington Square*. The portrait of James shows him at age seventy; it was done by John Singer Sargent.

ROBINSON JEFFERS
1887 — 1962
Sewickley, Pennsylvania

The first child of William Hamilton Jeffers and Annie Jefferson Tuttle Jeffers, Robinson Jeffers was born on Ridge Avenue, North Side, Pittsburgh in 1887. A short time later, William Jeffers built a home at 44 Thorn Street, Sewickley, about twelve miles from the Western Theological Seminary in North Side where he was a Professor of Old Testament Literature. He was also a frequent supply minister in the Presbyterian Church, Sewickley, a lovely residential area where Mrs. Jeffers' cousin, a Mr. Robinson, lived. Later on, the Thorn Street home was sold and the family bought "Twin Hollows," the Daniel E. Nevin estate in Edgeworth. Robinson Jeffers attended several private schools in Pittsburgh and its suburbs in addition to boarding schools in Switzerland and Germany. When his family returned from a lengthy stay in Europe, Jeffers attended the University of Western Pennsylvania for a year. In 1904 the family decided to move to California because of William Jeffers' health. Thus Jeffers' ties, interest, and love for California began.

HERMAN MELVILLE
1819 — 1891
Albany Academy, Albany, New York

In 1830 Herman Melville attended Albany Academy, located in downtown Albany, New York, in a park adjacent to the capitol building. In 1832 when his father died, however, he had to leave school because of financial difficulties. The old Academy building is now used for state offices, and yet as a reminder of Melville's family one may see there a portrait of one of the Gansevoorts, his mother's prestigious family. Whereas Melville knew a boyhood of ease and high expectations, being reduced to the status of a poor relative after his father's business failures and death, and finally having to ship out as a common sailor to earn money, cost him a great deal of hurt pride. The new Albany Academy is located outside of the city, on Academy Road; Herman Melville remains its most distinguished son.

Troy House

This white frame house is located at 114th Street, off Route 4, Troy, New York. At intervals Melville lived at the Troy House from 1838-1847 while he taught school. Since he had gone to sea when he was nineteen years old, he had many experiences as a merchant sailor. In 1841 he again shipped aboard a whaler bound for the Pacific and was gone for about four years. He made his way home by escaping to Tahiti, shipping on another whaler to the Hawaiian Islands and enlisting in the U.S. Navy. He was able to use these adventures with fictional license in his books *Typee* (1846) and *Omoo* (1847), the first modern novels of South Seas adventures. They were immediately popular because their subjects and settings were largely unknown to American and English readers.

JAMES MICHENER
1907 —

Reared in Doylestown, Pennsylvania, James Michener was graduated *summa cum laude* from Swarthmore College and received
a Master's degree from Colorado State College. He taught in a
private school for several years and was a visiting professor of
education at Harvard before enlisting in the Navy. Although he
had written articles that were published, his first novel *Tales of
the South Pacific* (1947) received the Pulitzer Prize, and in 1949
Rodgers and Hammerstein adapted it as the great musical play
South Pacific, one of the most often revived classics of music
theater. His huge novel *Hawaii* (1959) was on the best-seller lists
for twenty months with a sale of six million copies. It was trans-
lated into twenty-four languages. Michener was an ardent and
thorough researcher who went to the countries he wrote about
to learn as much as possible about the people and their cultures.
As a result, his writing is detailistic and accurate. In April 1967,
he received the Einstein Award of the Einstein Medical College
because of his interest in peace in the Middle East. Michener also
wrote *Return to Paradise* (1951), *The Bridges of Toko-ri* (1953),
Sayonara (1954), *Caravans* (1963), *The Source* (1965), *Quality
of Life* (1970), *The Drifters* (1971), and *Centennial* (1974); all
were best-sellers.

EDNA ST. VINCENT MILLAY
1892 — 1950
Steepletop

"Vincent," as she was called by her family and friends, lived in Camden, Maine when she was growing up and used its unique view of mountains and sea for her brilliant poem *Renascence*, published when she was only nineteen years old. After attending Vassar, attractive Vincent decided to become an actress, an unsuccessful plan. She went to live in Greenwich Village, New York, where she continued to write and produced a book of poetry, *A Few Figs from Thistles* with some poems about New York. Some of her other books are: *Second April, The Buck in the Snow,* and *Wine from These Grapes.* Vincent, a Pulitzer Prize winning poet, developed the quality of courage while she lived in Greenwich Village, the courage to live spontaneously, to love deeply, to feel grief and loneliness unashamedly. After her marriage to Eugen Boissevain, a Dutch merchant in 1923, Millay and her husband withdrew to the Berkshires at Steepletop (Austerlitz, New York) and to Ragged Island, off the Maine coast. Located on 700 acres, the Colony at Steepletop is now used for those who are interested in the arts.

EDGAR ALLAN POE
1809 — 1849
Philadelphia Home

Edgar Allan Poe's House, once called the "rose-covered cottage," is located at 530 North 7th Street, Philadelphia. The restored home is separated from a newer building by a stairwell. In the living room Poe did his writing as well as entertaining his friends. He had a study on the second floor. Poe's mother-in-law Mrs. Clemm, who served as housekeeper, also helped to nurse Poe's wife Virginia during her many illnesses. Meanwhile, Poe kept writing not only for survival but also to pay for the many medical bills. He had come to Philadelphia in 1839 to be editor of *Burton's Gentleman's Magazine.* During his two years in the cottage he was a prolific writer, producing "The Gold Bug," "The Masque of the Red Death," "The Pit and the Pendulum," and many other renowned short stories. Though he is equally famous as a writer of short stories and poems, Poe is best-known for that show-piece and tour de force of all poetry, "The Raven." The "lost Lenore" of the poem may refer to his slowly dying wife Virginia, to some earlier sweetheart, or to a composite view of Poe's favorite theme in verse and prose, the death of a beautiful woman. Written in the Philadelphia house, "The Raven" was revised a number of times. Some critics do not take Poe very seriously; Lowell called him "three-fifths genius and two-fifths sheer fudge." French poets and critics were enthralled by Poe; Baudelaire and others were inspired by his writings when they created the Symbolist movement. At any rate, Poe's works are classics of a special kind, regardless of how badly they have been exploited in grade B movies and television shows. One of the marks of a great classic is to be badly imitated many times over. Justly famous for his strangely evocative poems and for his tales of terror, Poe also deserves to be remembered as the inventor of the detective story.

W. D. SNODGRASS
1926 —
Home, Beaver Falls, Pennsylvania

When Dewitt, as he is called, was one year old, his family moved from Wilkinsburg to Beaver Falls, Pennsylvania and established the family home at 3121 Fourth Avenue. The three-story brick structure sitting on a corner can be recognized by the two catalpa trees the poet describes in his poem "April Inventory." Only one block away is Geneva College, which Dewitt attended for one year. After serving in the Navy he completed his education at the University of Iowa. He has taught at Cornell, University of Rochester, Wayne University, and is now at Syracuse University. In 1960 he was awarded the Pulitzer Prize for his book of poetry *Heart's Needle*, which is primarily autobiographical; in fact, the title is taken from a phrase found in an old Irish story, "An only daughter is the needle of the heart." Snodgrass was thinking about the very difficult period of a father's relationship to his little girl while he is divorcing and remarrying. Snodgrass has received many awards and honors and has frequently represented the United States as a cultural ambassador sent by the State Department, as in his trip to Russia. On a Guggenheim Fellowship he was in Germany for a time, and he was inspired to write and develop into a play *Führer Bunker*, twelve booklets about Hitler's life. His book *Gallows Songs* consists of translations of German poetry, and *After Experience*, poems and translations, was taken from direct experiences; it deals in part with the works of several great painters. With his dedicated interest in music, the poet has displayed remarkable insight on the interplay of fine painting and music and fine painting and poetry.

WALLACE STEVENS
1879 — 1955

Wallace Stevens was born in Reading, Pennsylvania at 323 North Fifth Street. He attended high school in Reading, went to Harvard and was graduated from New York Law School. Although he practiced law in New York, after five years he joined the legal staff of the Hartford Accident and Indemnity Company and was transferred to Hartford, Connecticut. Meanwhile he married Elsie Viola Kochel, a Reading girl, and continued the writing career he had begun in high school. His poems began to appear in magazines such as *Poetry*, and his play *Three Travellers Watch a Sunrise* was produced at the Provincetown Playhouse in New York. A sampling of his poetry books includes *Ideas of Order*, *Harmonium*, *Collected Poems*, and *Opus Posthumous*. He began to appear on college campuses to read his poetry, was named Vice President of his insurance company, and declined Harvard's offer for him to accept the Charles Eliot Professorship of Poetry. In 1955 Stevens won a Pulitzer Prize for his *Collected Poems*. True enough, he is a poet's poet, one who uses language of ambiguity and obscurity; but he has a "rage for order" that he tries to create through words. Stevens once remarked that poetry "is not a literary activity; it is a vital activity." Definitely chauvinistic, Stevens has filled his poetry with American scenes, places, persons. His associates in the insurance industry never suspected he was also a poet, and yet he himself saw no conflict between the two occupations: he took Benjamin Franklin, the all-around man, as his ideal.

MARK TWAIN
1835 — 1910
Portrait

During his prosperous Hartford years and summers spent at Quarry Farm in Elmira, New York, each day Twain put on a freshly laundered white linen suit, the epitome of his idea of a Southern gentleman. The distinctive mop of white hair is also part of the image, but when he was a boy it was red and very curly, much to his dismay, and he would soak the unruly mass at the pump and try to plaster it down in place.

Mark Twain's Study, Elmira, New York

The Mark Twain Study is a replica of a Mississippi river boat pilot house. Twain had it especially built at Quarry Farm in Elmira, New York, to recall his days as a river boat pilot on the Mississippi (1857-1861). Doing a great deal of his summer writing in the "pilot house," he could find privacy and quiet away from his family and guests at Quarry Farm. The small structure is now located on the campus of Elmira College. Although Twain moved from Elmira to Hartford in 1871, his summers were still often spent at Quarry Farm. The family was there in 1880, for example, and young Rudyard Kipling sought out Twain at Quarry Farm in the summer of 1889 or 1890.

Grave of Samuel Langhorne Clemens (Mark Twain)

Mark Twain is buried with his family in Woodlawn Cemetery, 1200 Walnut Street, Elmira, New York. Twain's grave reads, "Samuel Langhorne Clemens — Mark Twain — Nov. 30, 1835 — April 21, 1910." Twain wrote the inscriptions for the graves of his wife Olivia and their children. Olivia's grave reads, "In this grave reposes the ashes of Olivia Langdon/ the beloved and lamented wife of Samuel L. Clemens/ who reverently raises this stone to her memory." Twain's daughter Clara Clemens erected a Mark Twain-Gabrilowitsch monument in honor of her father and her first husband, who wanted to be buried at the foot of Mark Twain.

JOHN UPDIKE
1932 —

Whereas some American authors are obsessed with moving about (Crane, Hemingway), John Updike has written his loyal best about his boyhood environment, Shillington, Pennsylvania. The town is called "Olinger" in the stories and novels. Updike writes about the Depression experiences of his childhood, about his growing up during the Second World War, and he writes with a special fondness for details about middle America. He does not mythologize "place" the way Faulkner does; somewhat in the way

of William Dean Howells, an earlier American realist, he takes
common things like the smell of a vacant high school classroom,
or the way a girl's knee feels next to his own in the booth at a
soda fountain, and finds in the release of such ordinary matters
his own subject. As a *summa cum laude* Harvard graduate in 1954
and continuing contributor to *The New Yorker* he has remained
loyal to his subject, middle America, and to his particular style
of Christian faith. *The Centaur* (1964) is a moving portrayal of
a high school teacher as seen through the eyes of his son, a high
school student. *Rabbit Run* (about the 1950's) and *Rabbit Redux*
(about the 1960's) deal with non-hero Harry Angstrom whose
past as a high school basketball star finds in his young or middle
manhood no ready substitute for that brief splurge as a golden
boy shooting baskets for his team.

WALT WHITMAN
1819 — 1892
Portrait

The portrait of Whitman is an oil painting on wood. The original, done to celebrate the poet's fifty-sixth birthday, is found in
the Walt Whitman House, Mickle Street, Camden. It contrasts
remarkably with the early portrait of Whitman printed in the first
edition of *Leaves of Grass* in lithograph form: this important
book was published within a day or two of July 4, 1855, and it
did indeed declare American poetry forever free of British and

European conventions. The portrait in this book shows Whitman at age thirty-six with a dark, short-trimmed beard, a black fedora hat and his head at a casual tilt; his workingman's shirt is open at the collar, his left hand in its pocket and the right one fisted against his waist, the elbow out. The later oil portrait, as well as photographs of him in old age, are dominated by the benignant white hair and full beard, but the lithograph of the young man shows the poet at "ease," who "loafs" and is at once "Myself" and all of humanity, all key words in his "Song of Myself."

Whitman's Home, Camden, New Jersey

The celebrated American poet Walt Whitman lived at 330 Mickle Street, Camden, New Jersey, where he spent the last years of his life, 1884-1892. A national landmark, the house is located in center city. Best known for his monumental book of poetry *Leaves of Grass*, Whitman devised a "free verse" with varied lines and rhythms and an extraordinary range of subject matter. It provided an example that slowly communicated itself to other poets who wanted to refresh the art. Whitman was a visionary poet emphasizing not only "a simple separate person" but also all of mankind. His Camden house, the only home he ever owned, contains furnishings, books and mementoes. There are also personal artifacts, facsimile manuscripts and various editions of the poet's works, such as *Leaves of Grass*, which went through many editions. One can also see Whitman's rocking chair, the knapsack he used to peddle his books, and his bath tub. Whitman loved ferries (see his poem "Crossing Brooklyn Ferry"), and he was ferrying one day when Henry Wadsworth Longfellow came to see him. But many writers, such as Twain, James, Stevenson, Holmes and Whittier, paid him visits of homage. Because of his meager earnings and his physical disability, they gave him a horse and buggy which he loved to race around Camden. Two miles away is Harleigh Cemetery, where Whitman and most of his family are buried in a mausoleum designed by Whitman.

Whitman, Stafford House
Laurel Springs, New Jersey

This marker reads, "A Pleasant House, part of it quite old, with maples and lilac bushes growing in the yard." The house was Walt Whitman's summer home, where he lived 1876-1881. In this home located at 315 Maple Avenue, Laurel Springs, New Jersey, he worked on his last edition of *Leaves of Grass* and *Specimen Days*. The house was owned by Harry Stafford, who in 1876 invited his friend Whitman to spend a weekend there. Whitman stayed all summer and many summers thereafter while he tried to recover from a stroke. He loved the rustic atmosphere as he relaxed and enjoyed the streams, birds, flowers and trees — a bit of nature away from the busy waterfront city of Camden where Whitman's home was located. In Timber Creek near the Stafford House, Whitman loved to bathe and sit.

WILLIAM CARLOS WILLIAMS
1883 — 1963
Rutherford, New Jersey

Pediatrician and writer, William Carlos Williams was able both to integrate this unlikely duo of professions and also to treat them as separate entities. At one time, he said "One feeds the other, in a manner of speaking." His patients were chiefly families of industrial workers who lived in his town of Rutherford (called Paterson in his poems), New Jersey, an industrial city on the Passaic River with a population reflecting an American racial and cultural mix. (He delivered more than 2,000 babies in and around Rutherford.) Because of his intimacy with the city, he was interested in writing *Paterson*, in four books. It was his major poetic work, his "personal epic." The poem, reflecting his home, profession, and country, is a long narrative based on the historical and social background of Paterson. Thus the focus of his poetry is the provincial life of the Eastern seaboard, with his interest in small towns, suburban roads set in neat grass plots and other roads that permitted him in between his doctoring and writing to escape to Manhattan to visit with others who were interested in writing, painting, photographing, sculpting. His own exhibits, which included paintings, sculptures, drawings, photographs, prints, as well as poems and books, combined his "painterly vision" effectively and accurately. His best known single poem, "Tract," was read by his minister as a final goodby at the side of Williams' own grave. It gives instructions to his townspeople on "how to perform a funeral." With mock humor and mock anger, he presents the materialistic view of a funeral: the hypocritical devices used to hide grief. He recommends avoiding formality and superficiality and reverting to simplicity. Influenced by Ezra Pound, his language is accurate and idiomatic.

SOUTH

STEPHEN CRANE
1871 — 1900
New Smyrna Beach, Florida

When he was only twenty-eight (the year before he died) Crane had written so much that it fills a dozen volumes in the collected edition of his works — all this plus some highly venturesome experiences that range from war reporting to living with down-and-outers in New York's Bowery. A preacher's kid, he had little use for the parental Methodism or any other religious orthodoxy. His highly realistic novel *Maggie: A Girl of the Streets* (1893) was unpopular because readers wanted saccharine romances. *The Red Badge of Courage* (1894) is an even more surprisingly modern book: it puts war in a 20th century light and views Henry Fleming, its hero, as a highly complex being with ambiguous motives. Once and for all, Crane put an end to the false stereotypes about heroism in battle. Also remarkable is the fact that Crane created the illusion of immediacy in this novel out of tales and anecdotes he gathered from Civil War veterans: he was too young to have experienced that war. *The Red Badge* brought Crane international fame, when he was only twenty-four. He constantly sought experiences in his travels — as on his tour of the West and Mexico. In the winter of 1896-97 he shipped on the *Commodore* as a war reporter to cover the insurrection against Spain in Cuba (an event staged by American yellow journalist publishers), but the munitions-heavy vessel sank eighty miles off Jacksonville, Florida on January 2. In a ten-foot dinghy, Captain Murphy, Crane, the ship's cook, and the oiler spent the next day and night in the stormy waters, not daring to attempt the surf near shore. The little boat came toward New Smyrna, Mosquito Inlet, and the Ponce Inlet Lighthouse (which is still standing). After running the surf at what is now Ocean Avenue, the dinghy was finally beached. Bystanders on shore never realized the men were in distress. Billy the oiler was smashed to death by the overturned boat; the others survived. That whole adventure is brilliantly fixed in Crane's story "The Open Boat." But Crane was off shortly to cover the war in Turkey, and later, the Spanish-American War: the substance of these lessons being that war is sickening and inglorious. Tuberculosis and malaria contracted at this time led to Crane's death after he had spent a short time living in England.

WILLIAM FAULKNER
1897 — 1962
Portrait and Rowan Oak, Oxford, Mississippi

"Mankind will prevail," the memorable phrase from Faulkner's 1950 acceptance speech for the Nobel Prize in Literature, persists as a theme in his fiction as his characters persist against odds that are sometimes ludicrous, sometimes tragic, sometimes impossible. Throughout the novel *Light in August* Lena Grove patiently trudges along country roads to find the father of the child she has conceived. The hard-luck family of Addie Bundren finally manage to get her coffined body to the town cemetery in *As I Lay Dying*. And of the black people listed in the addendum to *The Sound and the Fury*, Faulkner says, "They endured." Nearly all of Faulkner's novels and stories deal with a fictional county of Mississippi named Yoknapatawpha; Faulkner even did a map of it. The "real" county is Oxford, where Faulkner grew up and spent much of his life. *The Sound and the Fury* (1929) is his first important, and perhaps his greatest, novel; but the large body of his work, its innovative styles, its complex handling of themes, its extraordinary characterizations, have won this author international praise as the most important American novelist of this century. Since his fiction writing did not earn him an adequate income, he worked at intervals in Hollywood writing scripts (1936, 1939, 1944, 1946) and was well paid for these efforts. Nevertheless, his resources were strained by the restoration of Rowan Oak. A run-down antebellum house one mile outside of Oxford, Faulkner bought it in 1930 and lived there for the rest of his life. Being a fair carpenter, he did most of his own repair work. Modestly furnished, his study was at the rear of the house. Most noteworthy in this room is the outline of his novel *A Fable* (1954) written on the wall above one of the beds. Faulkner's expertise with American colloquial speech follows the precedent of Twain's *Huckleberry Finn*, and his rhetoric is the heir of Melville's *Moby Dick:* these are the most important American novels of the 19th century. Robert Frost once remarked that Russians wrote the best novels because Russian history has more pain and suffering than that of other nations. Faulkner, as heir to the suffering and defeat of the South in the Civil War, has by this measure enriched our literature with fiction that is not, for all its loyalty to place, parochial, but for all humankind.

ERNEST HEMINGWAY
1899 — 1961
Home in Key West, Florida

Ernest Hemingway's homes in Ketchum, Idaho; Key West, Florida; and Havana, Cuba represent the range of his experiences, and yet for all their differences they form a kind of composite of his character. From 1931-1961 Hemingway owned the Key West house where he wrote *For Whom the Bell Tolls, Green Hills of Africa, A Farewell to Arms, The Fifth Column, The Snows of Kilimanjaro,* and "The Short Happy Life of Francis Macomber." *To Have and Have Not* is Hemingway's "Key West" novel, though he wrote major portions of other works here as well. The Key West house was built in 1851 by Asa Tift, a wealthy Connecticut shipbuilder, for his young bride. When Hemingway and his second wife Pauline first came to Key West in 1928, the house was empty and rundown. Their first son Patrick was born in the year they came to Key West; Gregory was born after they moved into the house, which is located at 907 Whitehead Street. Hemingway's writing studio was on the upper floor of the adjacent, former carriage house, also used as a guest cottage. As early as 1939 Hemingway visited Ketchum, as a tourist. In 1941 he and his actor friend Gary Cooper were there. Then again in 1946 they were there to view the film version of *The Killers*; Hemingway was now married to Mary Welsh. In 1958, Cuba no longer appealed to Hemingway, and he returned to Ketchum. With civil war in

Cuba, life at his Finca Vigia home there was no longer safe or possible. Upon a final return to Ketchum in June 1961 (Ernest often traveled), he took his own life with a gun in much the same manner that his father had done in 1928. Finca Vigia, the Hemingway estate in Havana, is scarcely accessible today. Unfortunately, Hemingway's books and papers there are deteriorating badly because of heat, mildew, and neglect.

Studio, Home in Key West

Hemingway's studio room, which comprises the upstairs of the guest house adjacent to the main dwelling, was the place for writing during his Key West years, 1931-1940. He did not actually sell the Key West House; it was disposed of after his death in 1961. Martha Gellhorn came to Key West in 1936 with her mother; the upshot was that she interviewed him there, and was with him in Spain in 1937 doing film footage for a propaganda piece, *The Spanish Earth*. Divorce from Pauline and marriage to Martha occurred in 1940, the same year in which *For Whom the Bell Tolls* was published, a novel about the Spanish Civil War. The Key West studio room has louvred windows on every side, and the floor is paved with red Cuban tile. Ernest's life at Key West ended in 1940 with his divorce from Pauline, who continued to live in the house with their sons. Ernest and Martha moved to Cuba and the Finca Vigia. That marriage ended in 1945; in the next year Ernest married Mary Welsh, who is still living. It was

Mary and Charles Scribner, Jr., who assembled Ernest's manuscript for *Islands in the Stream* (1970), the legendary work which Ernest said he kept in a safe deposit box in Havana as assurance against the day when he could no longer write. It deals with Bimini and Cuba, and actions against German U-boats in World War II. One theory holds that the subject was so painfully autobiographical that Hemingway found it impossible to complete this work. The novel deals with the estrangement between the hero, Thomas Hudson, and his three sons — and his attempts to overcome it.

CARL SANDBURG
1878 — 1967
Connemara, Flat Rock, North Carolina

The Carl Sandburg Home in Flat Rock, North Carolina, is a National Historic site; Sandburg lived here with his family from 1945-1967, the year of his death. The farm at Flat Rock, twenty-five miles southeast of Asheville, contains 240 acres; it was called Connemara. Once the home of E. G. Memminger, Treasurer of the Confederate States of America, Connemara was sold to the National Park Service in 1969. Sandburg is famous for his poetry written in the style of Walt Whitman and for his distinguished biography of Abraham Lincoln, which was published in six volumes (1926-1939). His favorite preoccupation in earlier years was strumming a guitar and reciting his folk poetry, or that of others. As a young man he was a soldier, dishwasher, barbershop porter and farmhand; he worked on a railroad construction gang in Illinois, and yet he amazed the nation with *Chicago Poems* (1914, 1918, 1920, 1922). Of Robert Frost, his senior by only three years and his only challenger for the title of America's poet laureate, Sandburg said that their politics differed vastly: Frost was a Republican, and Sandburg a Socialist. Perhaps Sandburg's best effort to express the Populist view is his *The People, Yes* (1936), the book his wife said epitomized his philosophy.

THOMAS WOLFE
1900 — 1938
The Thomas Wolfe Memorial
Asheville, North Carolina

A man of gargantuan appetites, Thomas Wolfe was also gargantuan in his literary outpourings. But with the help of Aline Bernstein, and of Maxwell Perkins, the superb editor of Scribners publishing house, Wolfe's enormous output was shaped into novels of compelling force and power. After the success of *Look Homeward Angel* (1929) and *Of Time and the River* (1933), however, Wolfe broke off with Perkins and Scribners and turned to another editor and publisher. For some readers, the next two novels *The Web and the Rock* and *You Can't Go Home Again* (both published posthumously) were lesser works. Yet all the novels are a deep probing of Wolfe and people he knew well, initially those of Asheville, North Carolina (called Altamont in the books). Like Wolfe's father, Oliver Gant in the first novels is a stonecutter; and Wolfe's mother is shown through Eliza Gant, manager of a residential boardinghouse. The house which may be seen in Asheville is furnished with original family possessions. Originally called Dixieland, it preserves an instant recall of the cheap propriety and sparse discomfort that Wolfe furnishes it with in his novels. Now identified as The Thomas Wolfe Memorial, the house is located at 48 Spruce Street, Asheville, North Carolina. At his death, Wolfe left behind an eight-foot stack of manuscripts from which the last two novels were produced. Max Perkins, who was also Scribners' editor for Hemingway and Fitzgerald, said that Wolfe needed no biography: everything he wrote *was* about himself. If not true in literal detail, that statement is nevertheless true in a broad, emotional sense.

MIDWEST

SHERWOOD ANDERSON
1876 — 1941
Family Home, Clyde, Ohio

Where the Anderson family lived when Sherwood was growing up has many answers. The father Irwin's profession as handcraft harness-maker doomed the family to chronic failure and periodic moves from one house to another in the Ohio towns of Clyde and Elyria. In the two-story frame house located at 129 Spring Avenue, Clyde, the family lived longer than in any other of their five residences. According to Thaddeus Hurd, his father Herman said that Sherwood dug a cave behind the house with room for only two boys. Herman went there and received the secret initiation into the blood-fraternity. The porch was on the north side of the house. Beside the dwelling was a spring, a landmark where the Andersons and many other townspeople got their water. Here Emma the mother did laundry to earn money, just as Sherwood, the third child of six, tried his hand at many tasks and won the nickname of "Jobby" Anderson. Irwin drifted more and more to drinking and idleness, but his knack for storytelling was a gift inherited by Sherwood, whose episodic novel *Winesburg, Ohio* gathers nostalgic tales about small-town disappointments and foolish hopes. At the end of the novel the young hero, newspaper reporter George Willard, boards the train to Chicago more or less as Anderson himself left the small towns to become one of the Chicago Renaissance writers. Anderson's characters, who are frustrated as they fight against conventionality, are constantly seeking solutions and escapes. He is often linked with the novelists Dreiser and Lewis, and the poets Lindsay and Masters; but he was also influenced by Gertrude Stein and James Joyce. A better writer of short fiction than of novels, Anderson's stories have been paid the supreme tribute of being imitated by Ernest Hemingway. Anderson also knew and advised William Faulkner in New Orleans in 1925, when Faulkner was writing his first, unsuccessful novels.

ERNEST HEMINGWAY
1899 — 1961
Oak Park, Chicago

Ernest Hemingway spent his life alternating between colorful, heroic experiences and writing about those experiences. *The Sun Also Rises* (1926), his earliest and best book, is about events and people in Hemingway's own life in Paris and Spain, events of just a few years earlier. Some of the characterizations seemed ungenerous, even libelous, to the real persons; and yet this classic novel speaks better than any other book for the disillusioned Lost Generation of post World War I. Similarly, Ernest's life had been full of frustrations and disillusionment. Part of his boyhood was ruled by the stuffy propriety of Oak Park, Chicago, and the rules of Grace his mother, a concert singer. The other half enjoyed the freedom of hunting and fishing with his father Dr. Hemingway in upper Michigan. The "bitchiness" of some of Hemingway's women characters probably derives from Ernest's resentment of his domin-eering mother (note Mrs. Macomber); and the pitiable weakness of some of the male characters (note Robert Jordan's father) is probably due to Ernest's perception of Dr. Hemingway. As a war reporter, Hemingway helped "liberate" Paris in World War II; and as a volunteer ambulance driver for the Italian Army in World War I, he received the shrapnel leg wounds that are reexpressed in various ways in various of his novels and stories. Hemingway celebrates the contests of sportsmanship in big game hunting on

African safari, in the rivalry of man and beast in the Spanish bull ring, in the match of strength and skill between marlin and fisherman in the Caribbean. He was contemptuous of men who lacked the courage and skill to compete in such contests, and he was contemptuous of writers who romanticized or falsified life. (He despised W. H. Hudson's idealized pictures of South America, and he ridiculed F. Scott Fitzgerald's accounts of rich people.) For Hemingway, the perfected ritual of the matador Romero courting violent death was a discipline like the one which he strove for in his own writing. "Grace under pressure" describes the Spartan agility of his prose style and (at its best) his life style. When guilty of pointless violence and meanness in his own life, he was expressing frustration over his own failure and that of others to live by that style.

ABRAHAM LINCOLN
1809 — 1865
Home in Springfield, Illinois

Abraham Lincoln came to Springfield, Illinois, in 1837 as a law partner of John Todd Stewart, although three years earlier he had been a state representative in the Illinois General Assembly and had helped to choose Springfield as the site of the state capital. Lincoln confronted Stephen A. Douglas in the State Senate, lost his place to Douglas in 1858, and in turn defeated Douglas in 1860 in the contest for the presidency. Also in Springfield, Lincoln met his wife-to-be, Mary Todd. Distinguished for his simple but moving style of writing, as in the famous Gettysburg Address, Lincoln has been a favorite subject for important writers. The monumental biography of Lincoln by the poet Carl Sandburg is an important example. When Lincoln was leaving Springfield for Washington, D.C. to take up his new duties as President, he stood bareheaded in the cold rain and spoke to the people of his city: "To this place, and the kindness of these people, I owe everything . . . I now leave, not knowing when or whether ever I may return, with a task before me greater than that which rested upon Washington." That task was to lead a nation fatally divided over the issue of slavery. When he did return, it was by way of the flag-draped funeral train which Walt Whitman so eloquently describes in the greatest elegy in American literature, "When Lilacs Last in the Dooryard Bloom'd."

Lincoln died of gunshot wounds when lilacs were in full flower, and Whitman describes them as the floral tribute from the common people Lincoln loved.

VACHEL LINDSAY
1879 — 1931
Springfield Home

The sign before Lindsay's home reads: "Home of Illinois Poet/ Nicholas Vachel Lindsay/ 1879-1931/ Author of Children's Fantasies and Animal Poems/ Designer of symbolic censers, trees, flowers and butterflies./ Idealist stressing the importance of nature, beauty, human and civic values./ Preacher of a social philosophy relevant to today's broad world outlook." Lindsay was part of the movement of revolt developing before the First World War against industrialism and business values. He lived at 603 South Fifth Street, Springfield. The substantial home has been kept intact with many of the poet's books, paintings and drawings. Best known for his public appeal, Lindsay spent most of his time touring and reading his poetry. His poems "The Congo" and "General William Booth Enters into Heaven" lend themselves to background music and chanting, as heard in the recordings still found in his home. Since Abraham Lincoln also lived in Springfield, many people have read and admired Lindsay's poem "Abraham Lincoln Walks at Midnight." Although Lindsay attended Hiram College, Frank

Luther Mott, a University of Iowa professor wrote that Lindsay was a "bunker" in that he wrote extemporaneously on folk stories.

MARK TWAIN
1835 — 1910
Boyhood Home, Hannibal, Missouri

Mark Twain's boyhood home is a small two-story house located at 208 Hill Street in the Mark Twain Mall. Built in 1844 by Sam's father, it is unpretentious with small rooms and low ceilings. Although the family moved to the "Pilaster House" across the street in 1846 because of their small income, they returned to their original home after Sam's father died in 1847. Nearby is the famous Mississippi River, the subject of much of Twain's writing, the wonderful, exciting, romantic river of his boyhood. Here he received his education, learning from nature what he did not receive in a classroom. For a time, however, he was apprenticed to his brother Orion as a printer's assistant, setting type and doing odd jobs. Although he did not live in Hannibal much past his boyhood, the town and its environs provided the setting for many of Twain's books. Near the home are the Museum, the Becky Thatcher House, Tom Sawyer Dioramas and the famous Mark Twain Cave the author referred to in several of his books.

Tom Sawyer's Fence

Tom Sawyer's Fence, restored now, is found next door to Twain's boyhood home in Hannibal, Missouri. In *The Adventures of Tom Sawyer*, we find quickly enough that Tom hates work more than anything else in the world. When Tom's Aunt Polly tells him to whitewash the fence, he outwits her by conning his friends, like Ben, to take over the coveted job. Meanwhile, Tom sits in the shade and munches his apple. He even offers to show Jim his sore toe if Jim will help to paint the fence, but Aunt Polly intervenes. By mid-afternoon, nevertheless, Tom has become boy-wealthy because his friends have paid him for the privilege of whitewashing the fence. One of Hannibal's current traditions is a contest at white-washing the fence, just as Calaveras County, California, holds a jumping frog contest to commemorate Twain's story of the celebrated jumping frog.

WEST

WILLA S. CATHER
1873 — 1947
The Cather Home, Red Cloud, Nebraska

Although Willa Cather was born of an old Virginia family from the Shenandoah Valley, she and her parents moved to Nebraska in 1883 when Willa was just under ten years old. Coming to the rough unclaimed landscape of Red Cloud, her father told her that she would need "grit" to survive here. She did so, and memorialized in some of her best novels like *My Ántonia* (1918) the tough spirit of the western pioneers. The white story-and-a-half house of the Cathers on Third and Cedar Streets remains much as it was in Willa's day, even to the wallpaper she put on by herself in her upstairs dormer bedroom. Willa describes this house in her novel *The Song of the Lark* (1915) and in her stories "Old Mrs. Harris" and "The Best Years." The present house furnishings were chosen to suit the descriptions in the novel and stories. The Cather family lived here from 1884-1904.

Willa Cather belonged to the Episcopal Church of Red Cloud from 1922 until the time of her death. It is located at Sixth and Cedar Streets; one of its windows is dedicated to Willa's father and one to her mother. But in her childhood she heard sermons in various immigrant churches — Norwegian, Danish, Swedish, French Catholic, Czech, or German Lutheran. Though her family were Baptists, Willa's vital interest in different ethnic and religious groups made possible such novels, with their varied geographic and cultural settings, as *My Ántonia* (Nebraska), *Death Comes for the Archbishop* (New Mexico), and *Shadows on the Rock* (Quebec).

Burlington Depot, Red Cloud

Willa Cather's periodic returns to Red Cloud, whose name memorializes that of a famous Indian Chief, were always by way of the old Burlington Depot, built in 1897. Whether she was living in Pittsburgh, or later in New York City, or returning from Europe, Willa felt strong ties for the prairie town that was the locale of her appropriately-named story "The Best Years." Jim Burden, the narrator of the novel *My Ántonia*, also returns in midsummer by railroad to the prairie town of his youth, experiencing the heat and dust of the long trip and the heightened emotion of coming home again after a long absence: "We agreed that no one who had not grown up in a little prairie town could know anything about it. It was a kind of freemasonry."

Willa Cather Pioneer Memorial, Red Cloud

The brownstone-front building was constructed in 1889 by Governor Silas Garber on Webster Street, Red Cloud; Garber is recalled as Captain Forrester in Willa Cather's novel *A Lost Lady* (1923). Originally the Farmers and Merchants Bank, Garber's structure now contains the Willa Cather Pioneer Memorial, with mementoes from the Cather family, such as the enamel signboard for Mr. Cather's land office, as well as wax figure exhibits depicting scenes from Willa's fiction. One scene represents "The Sculptor's Funeral," a bitter and moving account of the dead sculptor's body being returned to Sand City, a town much like Red Cloud, that did not understand or appreciate the greatness of their native son. A compelling theme of Cather's fiction is the tug of war between parochial loyalties and the lure of travel and "foreign" culture. Perhaps the epigraph from Vergil cited by college professor Gaston Cleric in *My Ántonia* says it best: "I shall be the first, if I live, to bring the Muse into my country."

ROBINSON JEFFERS
1887 — 1962
Hawk Tower, Carmel, California

Robinson Jeffers, who exploits the Big Sur setting of California in his poetry, built Tor House and Hawk Tower at what is now 26304 Ocean View Avenue, Carmel. Hawk Tower is nearly forty feet tall and is made of sea-worn boulders Jeffers rolled up from the beach and hoisted in place on a hand-built derrick. The tower was built especially to honor Una, Jeffers' wife, who was fascinated by the ancient stone towers of Ireland the couple saw while traveling there. The key-stone above the door of Hawk Tower has the letters "U" and "RJ" arranged in a triangle, and both Tor House and Hawk Tower feature unicorn motifs for Una. The first floor of the tower contains a primitively furnished workroom for Jeffers. On the second floor is a lovely small study, paneled in redwood, designed for Una. Jeffers fondly incorporated both in Hawk Tower and in Tor House fragments gathered on their travels: these structures contain stones from the Great Wall of China, the Pyramid of Cheops, Hadrian's Villa, and other famous monuments. On the third level of the tower, the turret, is a porthole from the ship *Inconstant*, wrecked in Monterey Bay in 1830; on this ship Napoleon escaped from Elba. Jeffers built Hawk Tower alone between 1920-1924. The Jeffers children loved to scramble up the narrow inner stone staircase. The tower captures some of the ruggedness and force that Jeffers sought to achieve in his poems

— qualities he believed modern poets were relinquishing to prose in favor of defeatism and eccentricity. In his view, the moderns had lost both physical and psychological reality. Hence, he turned to writing narrative poems expressing strong, compelling violence, such as *Tamar, Roan Stallion, The Tower Beyond Tragedy*, and *Give Your Heart to the Hawks*. Jeffers' adaptation of Euripides' *Medea* was done especially for Judith Anderson, whose performance in the lead role caught the sense of crisis and fateful disaster Jeffers believed essential to poetry.

Tor House, Living Room

Tor House, the home of Robinson and Una Jeffers, was built in segments over a period of time, with the aid of his twin sons when they grew older. Though Jeffers was over six feet tall, the ceilings of the rooms of Tor House are rather low — probably because the house faces directly on the ocean, and a taller structure would have been threatened by sea storms. Jeffers came to Carmel in 1914 and lived there until the time of his death in 1962. The area around the house was barren when he first came there, but now there are many large trees, including cypress, originally planted by the Jeffers family for privacy. A daughter-in-law still lives in a portion of Tor House, now modernized, although the house originally had only primitive facilities. The dramatic scenery of the Carmel coast attracted writers and artists to the area in the first decade of this century: Ambrose Bierce and Jack London, and later Sinclair Lewis,

Upton Sinclair, Lincoln Steffens, William Rose Benet. Like Steinbeck, Jeffers was interested in the forgotten older indigenous peoples of the California coast: hill people and herdsmen of Amerindian or Hispanic backgrounds. Into this culture Jeffers read an affinity with the primitivism of Greek tragedy which he pierced with insights from Freudian psychology. The living room of the original Tor House cottage displays some of Jeffers' favorite books and the small antique captain's desk where Una did her correspondence while Jeffers paced over the floorboards above creating poetry in the attic room. It was his habit to write each morning until lunch time; afternoons were for the garden or for stone masonry. In the garden may still be seen a small Roman statue of a boy riding a dolphin; it originally belonged to the American painter John Singer Sargent, who kept it in his garden in London.

JOHN STEINBECK
1902 — 1968
Family Home, Salinas, California

The Steinbeck House at 132 Central Avenue, Salinas, California, is the family home in which John spent his boyhood. Born in Salinas, he attended high school here and was graduated in 1919. He then went to Stanford University for five years but did not complete his studies. Nevertheless he secured many experiences working on neighboring Salinas farms with migrants. He also went to Oklahoma to learn more about the victims of the Dust Bowl of the 1930's who came to California in decrepit automobiles and broken-down trucks to become migrant workers in what they hoped, ill-advisedly, would be a Promised Land. It turned out to be nothing of the sort. Steinbeck told of their troubles in his novel *The Grapes of Wrath*, a work based on a series of newspaper feature stories he did on migratory workers. It was instantly popular, even notorious, and had considerable influence on legislation passed by Congress that attempted to deal with problems of the Okies and their like. The film version is a classic, starring Henry Fonda. Thus the Victorian upper middle class propriety of Steinbeck's boyhood home seems much at odds with the working-class sympathies of his fiction. Steinbeck House is now used as a tea room supported by the Valley Guild, a group of women whose purpose is to maintain the House. A basement room called "The Best Cellar" offers arts and crafts items for sale.

John Steinbeck Library, Salinas

At 110 West San Luis Street in Salinas, California, is the John Steinbeck Library with a large Steinbeck Memorial Room. When Steinbeck did research for his novel *East of Eden*, he worked in the old wing of this Library. Today the Steinbeck Room has manuscripts, first editions, photographs, and much memorabilia. Well-educated and well-read, Steinbeck used his knowledge of Greek and Roman history, medieval and Renaissance stories, and biological sciences in his novels. He once said that he never wrote two books alike. One will find this true if one reads *The Winter of Our Discontent*, *Sea of Cortez*, or *The Moon Is Down*. For artistic success, the best-known short story "The Red Pony" from *The Long Valley* shows Steinbeck's genius. Steinbeck was awarded the Nobel Prize for Literature in 1962.

Steinbeck Home, Pacific Grove, California

Steinbeck was familiar with Pacific Grove because he spent vacations there when he was young. Pacific Grove is located on the Monterey Peninsula near Cannery Row. In 1930, during his first marriage, Steinbeck and his wife lived at 147 Eleventh Street. The small reddish-brown three-room cottage was surrounded by tall pine trees. John loved this home which was only a few blocks from the ocean. It was enclosed by a high fence which shaded a lovely garden, a pond with turtles and water grasses. John and Carol lived in Pacific Grove for six years, then returned there at intervals. In 1948 after his second marriage had failed and he was separated from his two sons, he came back to Pacific Grove to enjoy his favorite house and to seek consolation. While he was here, in 1949 he met Elaine Scott, wife of Zachary Scott, who had a small daughter. She became his third wife after her divorce.

Cannery Row, Monterey, California

In Steinbeck's time canneries were needed since Monterey was a fishing and whaling center. Because of his interest in the area, Steinbeck wrote a novel called *Cannery Row*. In it, he refers to "Doc's Lab." "Doc" Edward Ricketts, a marine biologist who influenced Steinbeck with his philosophical ideas, lived at 800 Cannery Row. But Doc appears as spokesman for Steinbeck in many of his books. For example, Doc gives his social views in Steinbeck's novel *In Dubious Battle*, which is about an apple pickers' strike.

BIBLIOGRAPHY

Anderson, David D. *Sherwood Anderson.* New York: Holt, Rinehart and Winston, Inc., 1967.

Benedict, Stewart. *The Literary Guide to the United States.* New York: Facts on File, Inc., 1981.

Betts, Glynne Robinson. *Writers in Residence.* New York: The Viking Press, 1981.

Byrne, Kathleen D. and Richard C. Snyder. *Chrysalis: Willa Cather in Pittsburgh.* Pittsburgh: The Historical Society of Western Pennsylvania, 1982.

Chapman, Mary Lewis, ed. *Literary Landmarks.* Williamsburg, Virginia: Literary Sketches Magazine, 1974.

De Lana, Alice, and Cynthia Reik. *On Common Ground: A Selection of Hartford Writers.* Hartford, Connecticut: The Stowe-Day Foundation, 1975.

Edmiston, Susan and Linda D. Cirino. *Literary New York.* Boston: Houghton Mifflin Co., 1976.

Fenn, Mary R. *Tales of Old Concord.* [n.p.: n.p.], 1965. Privately printed for The Women's Parish Association, Concord, Massachusetts.

Gottesman, Ronald, *et al.*, eds. *The Norton Anthology of American Literature.* 2 vols., 1st ed. New York: W. W. Norton & Company, Inc., 1979.

Harting, Emilie C. *A Literary Tour Guide to the United States: Northeast.* New York: William Morrow & Company, Inc., 1978.

Jeffers, Donnan. *The Stones of Tor House.* [n.p.: n.p., n.d.].

Jeffers, Robinson, and Horace Lyon. *Jeffers Country.* San Francisco: The Scrimshaw Press, 1971.

Meltzer, Milton. *Mark Twain Himself.* New York: Bonanza Books, 1960.

Moore, Harry T. *Henry James and His World.* London: Thames and Hudson, Ltd., 1974.

Morrison, Kathleen. *Robert Frost: A Pictorial Chronicle.* New York: Holt, Rinehart and Winston, 1974.

Neider, Charles, ed. *The Autobiography of Mark Twain.* London: Chatto & Windus, 1960.

The Pennsylvania Council of Teachers of English. *Biographical Companion to the Literary Map of Pennsylvania.* [n.p.]: The Pennsylvania Council of Teachers of English, 1975.

Scherman, David E. and Rosemarie Redlich. *Literary America.* New York: Dodd Mead & Company, 1952.

Schmitz, Anne-Marie. *In Search of Steinbeck.* Los Altos, California: Hermes Publications, 1978.

Slote, Bernice, text; Lucia Woods *et al.*, photographs. *Willa Cather: A Pictorial Memoir.* Lincoln: University of Nebraska Press, 1973.

Stein, Rita. *A Literary Tour Guide to the United States: South and Southwest.* New York: William Morrow & Company, Inc., 1979.

_____. *A Literary Tour Guide to the United States: West and Midwest.* New York: William Morrow & Company, Inc., 1979.

ABOUT THE AUTHORS

Professors, writers, actors — Geri Bass taught English at Geneva College, Beaver Falls, Pennsylvania; Philadelphia College of Pharmacy and Science; Temple University; and Glassboro State University, New Jersey. Very active in community affairs, she has won many honors such as the Distinguished Service Award as Woman of the Year by the Upper Beaver Valley Jaycees. She has written and published poetry and has also edited publications like the *Keystoner*, journal of the Pennsylvania Division of the American Association of University Women.

Dr. Eben Bass, Professor of English at Slippery Rock University, Pennsylvania, has also taught at Ohio State University and the University of Pittsburgh. He has published poetry and many articles on Hemingway, James, Faulkner, Cather, Frost, Blake, Shakespeare, and Swinburne. His published book is *An Annotated Bibliography of Criticism of Aldous Huxley*. Because of his interest in drama, Dr. Bass has helped to direct Shakespeare and Classic Theater tours to Stratford, Ontario, sponsored by Slippery Rock University. He has given lectures on the relationship of classic films and the fine arts.

The Basses have traveled extensively for many years to secure the information they have incorporated in this book. In addition, they have given programs on Literary Landmarks, as well as dramatic dialogues on Emily Dickinson, Edna St. Vincent Millay, Sylvia Plath, and Dorothy Parker. The Basses have gathered a great deal of material on American writers who have traveled or have lived in Europe, for a book on American Writers in Europe.